William Ingraham Kip

History, object and proper observance of the Holy season of Lent

William Ingraham Kip

History, object and proper observance of the Holy season of Lent

ISBN/EAN: 9783337282851

Printed in Europe, USA, Canada, Australia, Japan

Cover: Foto ©ninafisch / pixelio.de

More available books at **www.hansebooks.com**

THE

HISTORY, OBJECT,

AND

PROPER OBSERVANCE

OF THE

HOLY SEASON OF LENT:

BY THE

Rt. Rev. Wm. INGRAHAM KIP, d. d.

BISHOP OF CALIFORNIA,

AUTHOR OF "THE DOUBLE WITNESS OF THE CHURCH;" "THE EARLY CONFLICTS OF
CHRISTIANITY;" ETC., ETC.

Twelfth Edition.

NEW YORK:

E. & J. B. YOUNG & CO.,

COOPER UNION, FOURTH AVENUE.

1881.

INSCRIBED

TO

THE RIGHT REVEREND

WILLIAM HEATHCOTE DELANCEY, D. D. LL. D.,

BISHOP OF WESTERN NEW YORK,

AS A SLIGHT TESTIMONY OF RESPECT AND

AFFECTIONATE REGARD

BY

THE AUTHOR.

O every where we find our suffering GOD,
    And where he trod
May set our steps: the Cross on Calvary
    Uplifted high
Beams on the martyr host; a beacon light
    In open fight.

To the still wrestlings of the lonely heart
    He doth impart
The virtue of his midnight agony,
    When none was nigh,
Save GOD and one good angel, to assuage
    The tempest's rage.

Mortal! if life smiles on thee, and thou find
    All to thy mind,
Think, who did once from Heaven to Hell descend
    Thee to befriend:
So shalt thou dare forego, at His dear call,
    Thy best, thine all.

KEBLE.

THE LENTEN FAST.

PREFACE.

For some years past each return of Lent has been, we believe, regarded with additional interest. Many who were not trained up within the pale of the Church, are looking to her fold as a refuge more fixed and stable than any they can find elsewhere. They of course eagerly inquire into the History, Object, and Proper Observance of the Holy Seasons which are set forth in her Calendar. Among those, too, who have been educated to attend her services, there seems to be a growing appreciation of their beauty, and a wish to know more of their origin. They appear to be turning away from the empty, boastful professions of this age of novelties, and to be more inclined to adopt as a settled principle, that golden decision of the Council of Nice, Εθη αρχαια κρατειτω, LET ANCIENT USAGES PREVAIL.

In this state of things, the writer has frequently sought—but without success—for something, which in a small compass might contain the necessary information with respect to the Lenten Fast. He could only find, a few pages by one author—a sermon by another—or perhaps some brief tracts, which, although excellent in themselves, did not attempt to discuss the whole subject. Having waited therefore for several years in vain, in the hope that the desired work would be furnished by some one better able to do it justice, he has at length ventured himself to undertake the task.

After the following pages were prepared for the Press, there was accidentally brought to his notice, a treatise by Dr. Gunning (afterwards Bishop of Chichester), entitled, " the Paschal or Lenten

Fast," which fills a quarto volume of between five and six hundred pages, published about the year 1670. Its size, however, together with the style in which it is written, would render it at the present day useless to any but the theologian or the scholar. The author has also confined his attention principally to one single point, owing to the circumstances under which he wrote. The work was prepared after the Restoration, when in consequence of the rule of the Puritans for so many years in England, the observance of Lent had been almost entirely discontinued. The object of Dr. Gunning is, therefore, to revive in the minds of men a reverence for this ancient season by proving its Apostolical authority; and the argument he presents is rendered most conclusive by extracts from every prominent writer who treats of the subject during the first seven centuries of the Church. It is evident however that this truth, if sustained by quotations from the

first three centuries, is as well established as if
the testimony of the remaining four was added.
The present writer found therefore, that even if
he had met with this treatise at an earlier period,
from its being thus narrowed down to a single
topic, it would have afforded him but little assistance.   He mentions it however in this place, as
it is the only work with which he is acquainted
devoted to this subject, and because he was happy to find in its numerous quotations, a full confirmation of the statement he had made with
regard to the origin of the Lenten Fast.

It would of course have been easy, after once
commencing the investigation, to have entered
more deeply into the subject and expanded this
volume to twice its present size by multiplying
quotations from the early writers.   In refraining
from doing so, and in turning aside from many
tempting paths of historical inquiry which opened
before him, the writer (although acting contrary

to the opinion of some of his friends), has been influenced by the consideration, that to have yielded, would entirely have changed the character of the work. It is intended, not for the clergy (for they must be professionally familiar with all it contains), but for those among the laity whose daily avocations prevent them from searching the early records of the Church and to whom information conveyed in this form is sometimes acceptable and useful. The object has therefore been, to quote from the ancient Fathers, merely enough to sustain and illustrate the different points brought forward.

It was for a similar reason that advantage was taken of the subject of Easter Even, to introduce a discussion of the intermediate state. Those arguments we already have, able as they are, seem rather too controversial and theological in their character to be adapted to general readers. An attempt has therefore been made, to present this important subject in a more simple and popular form. Perhaps exception may be taken by some, to the adoption of Bishop Horsley's rendering of 1 Peter, iii. 19, 20. If so, the writer can only say, that some years ago he himself thought differently, but after frequently studying this difficult point with all the help he could derive from the learned labor of others, he was finally obliged to settle down upon this interpretation, as giving the most natural explanation of the passage. It is the one adopted by Dr. Bloomfield and other eminent Biblical critics of the day. If, however, this passage should be entirely withdrawn from the argument the loss would not materially weaken it. There is, even without it, abundant Scripture evidence to prove the doctrine.

In conclusion then the writer would say, that it is with unfeigned diffidence he commits this little volume to the Press. Occupied with the engrossing cares of a parish, he has been obliged to prepare these pages almost entirely after the regular duties of the day were over, at night, and in times redeemed from sleep. Yet while engaged in the work, he has felt that such silent hours, when the noise and din of the busy city around had subsided into quietness, seemed an appropriate season in which to turn over those writings, bequeathed to us by the ages of a dim antiquity, and which we may well style—in Milton's eloquent language—"the precious life-blood of so many master spirits, embalmed and treasured up on purpose to a life beyond life." Their words, coming down through the mist and haziness of fifteen centuries, appeared to be gifted with a more touching emphasis when read in that still and solemn time, while the outward world, wrapped in slumber, gave no token of existence. To him therefore this labor has already brought its own reward. It has deepened his love and reverence for the Church at whose altars he is permitted to minister, and whose services he has here endeavored to illustrate. It has taught him to realize more fully than ever · before, the beauty of her ancient ritual, in which the solemnities of religion are performed — to use the words of Edmund Burke—" with modest splendor, with unassuming state, with mild majesty, and sober pomp."

If then the perusal of this little work should strengthen these feelings in the mind of any member of our Holy Apostolic Church, or awaken within one single soul which in uncertainty is " sounding on its dim and perilous way," the wish to turn to her as an Ark of safety, the writer will be most richly recompensed for all that he has done. If it can not thus aid the cause of truth and holiness, let it be like " the arrow shot into the air, which strikes no mark, creates no noise, leaves no track behind it, and is discovered after a little space, lying idly on the ground." But he hopes that this humble effort will not prove entirely in vain, and sends it forth therefore with the earnest prayer, that in some way it may be permitted to advance the glory of that Lord, whose blessed Passion the Church would solemnly commemorate on earth, while in Heaven a remembrance of its benefits will through all eternity furnish the theme for her noblest, loftiest anthem.

ASH WEDNESDAY, MDCCCXLIII.

CONTENTS.

O LORD, WHO FOR OUR SAKE DIDST FAST FORTY DAYS AND FORTY NIGHTS; GIVE US GRACE TO USE SUCH ABSTINENCE, THAT OUR FLESH BEING SUBDUED TO THE SPIRIT, WE MAY EVER OBEY THY GODLY MOTIONS IN RIGHTEOUSNESS AND TRUE HOLINESS, TO THY HONOR AND GLORY, WHO LIVEST AND REIGNEST WITH THE FATHER AND THE HOLY GHOST, ONE GOD, WORLD WITH-OUT END. AMEN.

COLLECT FOR THE FIRST SUNDAY IN LENT

THE OBJECT OF THE PRIMITIVE CHURCH IN INSTI TUTING THE HOLY SEASON OF LENT.

Welcome, dear feast of Lent! who loves not thee,
He loves not temperance, or authority,
    But is composed of passion.
The Scriptures bid us *fast;* the Church says *now;*
Give to thy mother, what thou wouldst allow
    To every corporation.

" *The Church,*" *by* HERBERT.

I.

OBJECT OF THE PRIMITIVE CHURCH IN INSTITUTING THE HOLY SEASON OF LENT.

At length the changing months have brought us to another division of our ecclesiastical year. We have again entered on that solemn season, in which the Church commands her children to "turn unto the Lord with all their hearts, and with fasting, and with weeping, and with mourning,"[1] — "worthily lamenting their sins, and acknowledging their wretchedness, that they may obtain of Him who is the God of all mercy, perfect remission and forgiveness, through Jesus Christ, their Lord."[2]   Her services now give utterance to the language of sorrow and abase-

[1] *Passage appointed for the Epistle for Ash-Wednesday.*
[2] *Collect for Ash Wednesday.*

ment, as we prepare for the solemn commemoration of our Lord's agony and death. It is interesting therefore to look back to the records of
he early Church in her holiest day, that as we
see the origin of this season, and the object for
which it was appointed, we may be enabled to
decide, whether we are so observing it, that it
shall answer for us its high and important pur-
poses.

The fast of Lent (a Saxon word, signifying
the Spring) is of forty days continuance, during
the six weeks which precede Easter. As however the Sundays are Festivals, and must therefore be excepted, only thirty-six days are left.
To make up this deficiency, four days are added
at the beginning, commencing with Ash-Wednesday,[8] which derives its name from the ashes
which in the ancient Church were at this time
thrown upon the penitents, whose sins had de-
barred them from a participation in her services.
" On the first day of Lent," says Gratian, in describing this ceremony, " the penitents were to

---

[8] It is uncertain by whom this addition was made.
Most writers, however, ascribe it to Gregory the Great.
(See BINGHAM'S *Orig. Eccles.*, lib. xxi., ch. 1, section 5).

present themselves before the Bishop, clothed with sackcloth, with naked feet, and eyes turned to the ground ; and this was to be done in the presence of the principal of the Clergy of the Diocese, who were to judge of the sincerity of their repentance. These introduced them into the Church, where the Bishop, all in tears, and the rest of the Clergy, repeated the seven penitential psalms. Then, rising from prayers, they threw ashes upon them, and covered their heads with sackcloth ; and then with mournful sighs declared to them, that as Adam was thrown out of Paradise, so they must be thrown out of the Church. Then the Bishop commanded the officers to turn them from the Church doors."[4] Severe indeed this discipline may seem ; yet in an age when the minds of men were reached only by striking appeals to the outward senses, we can not tell how much. these ceremonies may have availed to keep alive the purity of the Church, and to impress upon the careless multitude, the value of admission to her services.

An allusion to this ancient form is still pre-

---

[4] WHEATLY on *Common Prayer*, p. 233.

served in the "COMMINATION, or denouncing of GOD's anger and judgment against sinners," which in the service of the Church of England is commanded "to be used on the first day of Lent." After Litany the Priest is directed to say:

"Brethren, in the Primitive Church there was a godly discipline, that, at the beginning of Lent, such persons as stood convicted of notorious sin were put to open penance, and punished in this world, that their souls might be saved in the day of the LORD; and that others admonished by their example, might be the more afraid to offend.

"Instead whereof (until the said discipline may be restored again, which is much to be wished), it is thought good, that at this time (in the presence of you all) should be read the general sentences of GOD's cursing against impenitent sinners, gathered out of the seven and twentieth chapter of Deuteronomy and other places of Scripture; and that ye shall answer to every sentence, *Amen;* To the intent that, being ad monished of the great indignation of GOD against sinners, ye may the rather be moved to earnest

and true repentance; and may walk more wari-
ly in these dangerous days; fleeing from such
vices, for which ye affirm with your own mouths,
the curse of God to be due."

Then follow the anathemas, to which the people respond. This form has been omitted in the
Liturgy of the Church in America, with the exception of the three concluding prayers, which
on Ash-Wednesday are directed "to be said immediately before the General Thanksgiving."

All record of the precise time in which this
season first originated, is lost in the dim obscurity of the early ages of the Church. We may
therefore speak of its services, in the words with
which the ancient tragic poet represents Antigone as defending those sacred precepts of her
faith, which had come down upon the traditions
of a remote antiquity:

Ου γαρ τι νῦν γε καχθες αλλ' αει ποτε
ζη ταυτα κοὐδεις οἶδεν ἐξ ὅτου φανη.[5]

The Lenten fast is however frequently referred

---

[5] Not now, nor yesterday, but always thus
These have endured, their ancient source unknown.
SOPH. Antigone, 462.

2

to by writers of primitive days as an established and well known custom, which had been sanc‐ tioned by Apostolical authority. The probability is, that even from the first—from the time in which " the Bridegroom was taken away"—His followers thus in sorrow kept the anniversary of His Passion, although the duration of this sea‐ son, and the rules by which its observance was regulated, may not have been definitely settled until the age immediately succeeding that of the Apostles. Philo, who was cotemporary with the early disciples, and is even said " to have had familiar conversation with Peter at Rome, whilst he was proclaiming the Gospel to the inhabitants of that city,"[6] refers to this season in his descrip‐ tion of the Christians at Alexandria, who were converted by St. Mark. " This author"—says Eusebius, in his history composed about A. D. 324—" has accurately described and stated in his writings, the exercises performed by them," (i. e. the Christians of Alexandria in the days of St. Mark), " which are still in vogue among us at the present day, and especially at the *festival of our Saviour's passion, which we are accus‐*

[6] EUSEBIUS' *Eccles. Hist.*, liber ii., chap. 17, p. 66.

'omed to pass in fasting and watching, and in the study of the divine word. These are the same customs that are observed by us alone at the present day, particularly *the vigils of the Great Festival*,"[7] meaning by this the Passion Week, called by the Greek Fathers the Great Week.

It is also mentioned incidentally by Irenæus, who lived but ninety years after the death of St. John, and was trained up under the martyr Polycarp, who had himself been a disciple of that last surviving Apostle. When alluding to a difference of opinion with regard to the time in which it should be kept, he shows that the custom itself was ancient, even in his day. His words are: "This diversity existing among those that observe it, is not a matter that has just sprung up in our time, but long ago, among those before us."[8]

Tertullian too, who lived within one hundred years of the Apostle St. John's departure, has unwittingly as it were, recorded his testimony to the general belief of the Church in the Apostol-

---

[7] EUSEBIUS' *Eccles. Hist.*, lib. ii., chap 17, p. 68.
[8] *Ibid*, lib. v., chap. 24, p. 210.

ical Authority of this season. Having erred
from the faith, and embraced the heresy of the
Montanists, he found the voice of the Church
against him, when he endeavored to introduce
the new fasts which Montanus had commanded.
Thus therefore he argues against her authority,
in defence of his party. "They" (i. e. the Catholic Christians) "accuse us that we observe
fasts of our own, peculiar to ourselves. They
object therefore unto us novelty, and prescribe
against the unlawfulness of that, saying, it is
either to be judged Heresy, if presuming as men,
we so dogmatize, or we are to be pronounced
false prophets, if we inculcate these fasts, as from
the Spirit; whilst on either hand we hear them
denounce an anathema against us. For as to
what pertains to fast, they argue, *that there are
certain days constituted by God. They surely
think, that in the Gospel those days are deter-
mined for fasts, in which the Bridegroom was
taken away,* and that those days only are now
the legitimate days of Christian fasts, all legal
and prophetical old observances being antiquated
or abolished. Therefore as to other fasting, it is
to be indifferent, according to every man's occa-

sions and causes, at his own judgment, not of command." (That is, as Montanus inculcated the necessity of the fast, by pretended command from God.) "*And that thus the Apostles observed the rule of fasting*, imposing no other yoke of certain or set fasts to be kept of all in common. And ye prescribe against us, *that the solemn times for this matter, are to be believed already constituted in the Scriptures*, or in the tradition of our Elders, and that no further observance is to be superadded, for the unlawfulness of innovation."[9]

The first Christian Emperor, Constantine, immediately after the meeting of the earliest general council of the Church—that held at Nice, A. D. 325—and which was composed, to use his own words, " of all the Bishops, or the greater part of them at least, assembled together," wrote a letter to all the Churches, on the necessity of observing Easter upon the same day. His argument is, that unless this uniformity exists, some will be rejoicing in that Festival, while others are still mourning in the fasts which precede it.

---

[9] TERTULLIAN *De Jejuniis*, chap. 1, 2, 13.

" It is fit therefore "—he says—" that we should perpetuate to all future ages the celebration of this rite, *which we have kept from the first day of our Lord's passion even to the present times. . . . . . .* For the Saviour has bequeathed to us one festal day of our liberation, that is, *the day of His most holy passion;* and it was His pleasure that His Church should be one; the members of which, although dispersed in many and various places, are yet nourished by the same Spirit, that is, by the will of God. Let the sagacity of your holiness only consider how painful and indecorous it must be, for some to be *experiencing the rigors of abstinence,* and others to be unbending their minds in convivial enjoyments on the same day; and after Easter, for some to be indulging in feasting and relaxation while others are occupied in *the observance of the prescribed fasts.*"[10]

To give a single reference more — and they might be multiplied to a great extent—this· season is mentioned in the Apostolic Canons, a code of laws which certainly dates its authority from

---

[10] EUSEB. *De Vit. Constantin.* lib. iii., c. 17, 18. SOCRA·TES, lib. i.. chapter 6. THEODORET, lib. i., ch. 10.

a very early age. "If"—says the 61st Canon—
"any Bishop, Priest, Deacon, Reader, or Singer,
do not keep the holy fast of Lent, forty days before Easter, or the Wednesdays and Fridays, let
him be deposed, if he be not hindered by some
bodily infirmity; but if he be a layman, let him
be suspended from communion."[11]

Thus, we perceive, that this custom took not
its rise amidst the corruptions of the Dark Ages,
but began in times of light and holiness. We

[11] *Patres Apos.* COTEL. vol. 1, p. 451, *edit.* 1724. These
Canons have usually passed by the name of St. Clement.
Bellarmin, Baronius, and others, assert them to be the
genuine Canons of the Apostles. Cotelerius however ob-
serves, that the internal evidence is against this view of
their antiquity (*Jud. de Canon Apos.*, vol. 1, p. 429).
Hincmar, De Marca, and Beveridge give, what is the most
probable account, that they were framed by the Bishops
who were the disciples of the Apostles, in the end of the
2d and beginning of the 3d centuries. See BEVERIDGE *Jud.
de Can. Apos. in* COTEL. vol. 1, p. 436. See also, LARD-
NER's *Works*, vol. 4, p. 354. JORTIN's *Rem. on Eccles. Hist.*,
vol. 1, p. 278; CAVE's *Hist. Lit.*, vol. 1, p. 29. Even
Mosheim acknowledges that "they exhibit the principles
of discipline received in the Greek and Oriental Churches,
in the 2d and 3d centuries." (*Eccles. Hist.*, vol. 1, p. 90,
224). We give these authorities merely to show, that in
the lowest view taken of these Canons, they are good evidence of the practice of the Church at a very early age.

received it not from the Romish Church, when it
had fallen from ancient purity, but it comes
down to us from Primitive days. It was sanc-
tioned by Apostolical authority, or certainly at
least by those who lived before the example and
instruction of Apostles had been in any respect
forgotten. The early Christians, as we have already seen stated by Tertullian, considered our
Divine Master as referring to the observance of
some such season, when he said: "Can the children of the bride-chamber mourn, as long as the
bridegroom is with them? but the days will
come, when the bridegroom shall be taken from
them, and then shall they fast." At first, the time
of its observance varied in different Churches
and among different individuals, although all
agreed in the necessity of thus commemorating,
in some way, their Lord's sufferings and death.
At length, however, its duration was fixed at
forty days, which has since, through all the intervening centuries, continued to be the uniform
custom of the Church.[12] The number *forty* seems

---

[12] The question as to the length of Lent, at its first institution, is one which has caused much discussion among
learned men. The Greeks called this season Τεσσαρακοστη,

very anciently to have been appropriated to seasons of repentance and fasting. "This quadra-
gesimal number"—says St. Ambrose, in his 36th
sermon—" is not constituted of men, but consecrated from God." For this term of years were
the children of Israel disciplined in the wilderness, to prepare them for the promised land.
For forty days did Moses fast on the Mount—
Elijah in the Wilderness — and the Ninevites,
when they would avert the judgments prophesied
by Jonah. It was this length of time that our
Lord himself was pleased to fast, during His
temptation in the desert, and from his example
was this period probably fixed, " that, "— as
St. Augustine says — " we might, as far as we are
able, conform to Christ's practice, and suffer

and the Latins *Quadragesima*, both of which words denote
forty. But the inquiry has been, whether this applied to
days or hours? By some, it was argued, that it always
had been forty days. By others, that it at first extended
only through forty hours, which were of entire abstinence,
beginning about 12 on Friday, (the time of our Saviour's
falling under the power of death), and continuing until
Sunday morning, the time of His resurrection, and that
afterwards it was extended by the Church to the same
number of days. The reader will find this subject discussed in BINGHAM's *Orig. Eccles.*, lib. xxi., chap. 1

with Him here, that we may reign with Him hereafter."

And we may learn too from a single passage in St. Basil's Second Homily on Fasting, how universal throughout the world was the attention of the early Christians to this solemn portion of the Ecclesiastical year. " In this time of Lent, there is no island nor continent of the earth, no city, nor nation, no extreme corner of the world, where the Edict of this Fast of Lent was not heard. Yea, whatsoever armies, merchants, travelers, or mariners are abroad, this fast comes unto them all, and with joy they all receive it. This composes every house, every city, and every people, in sobriety and quiet and concord. This stills the late clamors, contentions, and noises of the town. Let no one, therefore, exempt himself from the number of the fasters, in which every degree, nation and age almost of men, and all of all dignities whatsoever are engaged."

How safe then are we, in yielding our ready obedience to this regulation of the Church! How much better, to tread in the footsteps of martyrs and confessors of former times, than to set at naught all the customs which they found conducive to their spiritual benefit, and to deter-mine — despising the wisdom of the past, and the recorded experience of eighteen centuries — to " walk every one in the ways of his own heart ! " It becomes therefore an inquiry of in-terest to us, gleaning from those ancient writers whose works have survived the ravages of bar-barism and the waste of time, to investigate the reasons which induced the Church in Primitive days to institute this Holy Season, and then through all succeeding ages, to insist so strongly upon its observance.

The first reason was — THAT HAVING THE SUB-JECT OF THEIR LORD'S SUFFERINGS THUS BROUGHT MORE VIVIDLY BEFORE THEM, THEY MIGHT BE INDUCED TO MOURN HIS LOSS WITH GREATER EARNESTNESS.

There is a tendency in the human mind to disregard a duty, to the performance of which no specific time is allotted. Thus, if the whole year were given us, during which we were com-manded at some period to meditate seriously on our Lord's death, we should probably either neglect the obligation entirely, or, at least, fulfil

it but imperfectly. It is for this reason that the
early Church set apart definite times, for considering in order each of the grand doctrines
of the Christian faith, as the Ecclesiastical year
rolls round. And in this practice we now continue.

> " Yes, if the intensities of hope and fear
> Attract us still, and passionate exercise
> Of lofty thoughts, the way before us lies
> Distinct with signs — through which in fixed career,
> As through a zodiac, moves the ritual year
> Of England's Church — stupendous mysteries!
> Which, whoso travels in her bosom, eyes
> As he approaches them, with solemn cheer." [14]

Beautiful indeed is that arrangement of her
services, which, as the months go by, brings in
succession before her Children, each scene in
their Lord's eventful life, and each cardinal truth
which he taught! We celebrate with joy and
gratitude the Festival of His Nativity, and afterwards follow Him on, step by step, through all
the glories and the trials of His earthly pilgrimage, until amid the solemnities of Passion Week
we mourn His agonies and death. Then come

[14] WORDSWORTH's *Eccles. Sonnets*, XV.

in meet succession, the other Festivals — that of
Easter, when He triumphed over the grave — of
the Ascension, when He returned to "the glory
which He had with the Father before the world
was" — and of Whitsunday, when His promise
was fulfilled, that the Comforter should be given,
and His Apostles, by the visible descent of the
Holy Ghost, were prepared to be "lights to
lighten the world." Thus it is, that in a far
higher and nobler sense than the Poet ever
dreamed in his loftiest imaginings—

"The rolling year is full of Him."

Acting then on this principle, and endeavoring
to render the views of her members clear and
distinct, how naturally did it happen, that one of
the first seasons of solemn remembrance instituted by the Primitive Church, was that which
commemorated her Lord's sufferings and death,
while her children were summoned in an especial
manner to lament those sins which brought Him
to the Cross!"[15] "The days had come, when the

---

[15] "It seemed good to the Church to fix a stated time,
in which men might enter on the great work of their repentance. And what time could have been selected with

Bridegroom was taken from them, and therefore did they fast." The memory of His love and kindness was still freshly imprinted on their hearts. The history of all that He endured, came not to them, as it too often does to us, like "a thrice-told tale," to which we have listened so often that it has lost its interest. The glad news of the Gospel bursting upon them in an age of moral degradation and darkness, had not yet ceased to thrill their hearts with joy. They had either "known Christ after the flesh," when in person he mingled with his fellow men, or at least those Apostles who sat at his sacred feet, forming His little household as He wandered through Judea; and with eager ears they listened to the recital from their lips, of all that they

greater propriety than this 'Lenten' or Spring Season, when universal Nature, awakening from her wintry sleep, and coming out of a state of deformity, and a course of penance, imposed for the transgression of man, her Lord and Master, is about to rise from the dead; and, putting on her garments of glory and beauty, to give us a kind of prelude to the renovation of all things? So that the whole creation most harmoniously accompanieth the voice of the Church, as that sweetly accordeth to the call of the Apostle, 'Awake, thou that sleepest, and arise from the dead, and Christ shall give thee light.'"—*Bishop* HORNE

had heard and witnessed. Probably too, the tradition of many a deed which is now lost forever, came down to them, and contributed to heighten their estimation of that Perfect Character, from whom they were separated by but a short interval of time.[16] How well then could they meditate upon His bitter agonies endured for them! How forcibly did they feel themselves called, once at least in each year, in an especial manner to chasten their souls by prayer and fasting, that they might thus be compelled to realize the nature of His earthly existence, who was truly "a man of sorrows and acquainted with grief!"

But if this was necessary for them, how much more so is it for us! Educated from the earliest dawn of reason, to hear the story of redeeming love, and the fearful manner in which our salvation was wrought out, these themes become to us, as we before remarked, subjects too well

[16] It is strange that the only one of these traditionary sayings of our Lord, which was afterwards recorded by an inspired writer, is intended to inculcate a truth, the most difficult for human nature to learn. St. Paul says— "Remember the words of the Lord Jesus, how he said: It is more blessed to give than to receive."—*Acts* xx. 35

known to excite attention. It is indispensable, therefore, that the mind should be directed and fixed upon them. And how admirably is this done by the appointed service of the Church! Week after week, we are led in her prayers and lessons to contemplate these solemn mysteries, until when Passion Week arrives, the recital is each day repeated. We witness the bitter agony of the Son of God, in the garden of Gethsemane. We stand by the patient sufferer's side, when arraigned in the hall of Pilate. We follow Him to Calvary, as he painfully toils along amidst the scoffs and jeers of an infuriated mob. We gather around the Cross, and hear that last expiring cry, which shrouded the heavens in darkness, and startled even the sleeping dead in their tombs. Hard, indeed, must be that heart—yes, utterly "past feeling"—which, amid scenes like these, is not awakened to gratitude and devotion. He can be no true follower of the Lord, whose spirit does not "burn within him" as he thus contemplates the mighty price at which his redemption was purchased, or whose resolution is not strengthened, to live for that Master who died a death of shame for him.

Another reason with the Primitive Church for the institution of this season was, TO AID HER MEMBERS IN PRESERVING THE HIGH STANDARD OF CHRISTIAN CHARACTER IN ITS EARLY PURITY. For a time, the followers of our Lord were subjected to the most painful persecutions. The lonely valleys of Judea furnished no place of security to the Hebrew Christians, for even thither penetrated their bigoted enemies, ready, "if they found any of that way, whether they were men or women, to bring them bound to Jerusalem." And when the faith left its earliest dwelling-place in "Holy Asia,"[17] and went forth

[17] ÆSCHYLUS' *Prom. Vinct.* 415, αγναςλόιας. This is the happy epithet used by the first, and may we not say, the loftiest of the Greek tragic poets? On this single point there is agreement between the Christian of every age, and the believer in that antique and poetical mythology which furnishes its inspiration to the muse of Homer, and both called into being, and imparted its dark coloring to the solemn and intellectual drama of the Athenian stage. Both alike look back with reverence to that region which was the birth-place of our race, the scene of its first revelations, and where "the Lord talked with man face to face." Even to this day, there is a tradition among the Arabs, that to the earliest places of human worship, there clings a guardian sanctity—that there the wild bird alights not and the wild beast may not wander—but the eye of God rests on them as hallowed spots.

to other lands, it found a world arrayed in hos-
tility against it.   The ancient, sensual Paganism,
and the proud systems of a scoffing philosophy,
united at once to crush that holy creed, which
disclaimed all fellowship with them.   The endur-
ance of its adherents was tried by every expe-
dient of cruelty their enemies could devise.
Some died in agony at the stake.   Some ascended to their reward from the burning flames, while
" their ashes flew, no marble tells us whither."
Some " butchered to make a Roman holiday,"
poured out their blood on the sands of the amphitheatre, welcoming even the wild beasts, whose
fury released them from their sufferings.   And
the survivors felt, that they also were each hour
in jeopardy of life, and might at any time be
called in like manner to seal their profession.
Yet these things only added a depth and fervor
to their devotion.   Like their Divine Master,
they " were made perfect by sufferings."   The
timid and wavering, either refrained from uniting
with them, or else soon apostatized from their
profession.   The true-hearted were therefore left
alone, reduced indeed in numbers, yet " steadfast, unmovable," and holding themselves ready,

if needs be, to win their crown by suffering the pains of martyrdom.

———————————— " Every hour,
They stood prepared to die, a people doomed
To death; old men, and youth, and simple maids."

The world looked coldly on them, even when it did not openly persecute, and had therefore nothing in it to enlist their affections. Life with them was one long Lenten period of abstinence and prayer, while they were continually chastening their spirits, to make ready for that parting hour, which might suddenly overtake them.

But when security came, and the world began to smile upon them, then was the time of peril. The faith which had been strengthening in the storm of persecution, drooped and withered in the sunshine of Imperial favor. The multitude insensibly declined from their Apostolic devotion, and thought too much of the cares and riches of a world they had vowed to renounce. Their affections began to cling to it, forgetting that here they were only strangers and pilgrims " having no continuing city." It was at this time probably that this fast, commenced in an earlier age,

was more accurately defined and inculcated by
the regulations of the Church, that her members
might be recalled from their secular cares to holy
works, and thus by the necessity of a law, compelled to dedicate one tenth of the year, in a
peculiar manner to their God.[18] Therefore it is,
that an ancient writer declares — " Whilst men
are distracted about the cares of this life, their
religious hearts must needs be defiled with the
dust of this world; and therefore it is provided
by the great benefit of this Divine institution,
that the purity of our minds might be repaired
by the exercise of these forty days, in which we
may redeem the failings of other times, and do
good works, and exercise ourselves in religious
fasting."[19]

But has this necessity in our day ceased ? Is
there now so great a deadness in the world, that
we need not such a season, to recall us to our
duty ? Is not the very reverse true, and the danger now tenfold greater than it was in that early
day ? Since all around us have made a nominal

---

[18] Cassian, in BINGHAM *Orig. Eccles.* lib. xxi. ch. 1,
sec. 10.

[19] Leo, Serm. iv., *de Quadragesima*, in BINGHAM, lib. xxi.

profession of Christianity, the Church has been too much mingled with the world. The barrier between them has been somewhat broken down, and there is comparatively but little of the out-ward Cross to be borne. But the effect of this is, to authenticate low views of Christian duty— to render religion earthly — to withdraw all attention from self-denial — to cause us to forget our Master's lesson, that though *in* the world we are not *of* the world—and to induce those about us to suppose that the "strait gate" has been widened, and the "narrow way" become broad. They look in vain for those exhibitions of a liv-ing faith which distinguished the early Christians, and are therefore tempted to believe, that the days of self-discipline are over, and an easier en-trance found into God's holy kingdom.

The very proofs too of Christian character — the marks by which we should ascertain our spiritual state — are in this age of novelties so perverted and mystified, that it is often difficult for an inquirer to decide, whether or not he has a right to those promises of the Gospel which are made to the contrite and believing. With some, every thing rests upon abstract notions of faith, as if the last Great Judgment would only be a trial of their orthodoxy. With others, all religion is resolved into a matter of mere feeling. Forgetting that the degree of excitement depends upon the power of the imagination, or the peculiar constitution of the mind, they are continually striving to elevate themselves to a greater intensity of emotion, and thus make this, intangible as it is, their test of religious character. The latter form of delusion indeed we may characterize as being in an especial degree, the popular one of the day. This awakening of the sensibilities and of the imagination, is substituted in the place of that calm, settled, decided resolution to obey the will of our Master, which alone can be an efficient rule of conduct in this evil world. These unearthly paroxysms of devotion, which soon pass away and leave behind them no abiding holiness, are trusted to, instead of that " patient continuance in well doing," which alone can lead us on to " eternal life." ·

How necessary is it then, that there should be times of reflection, when we may realize what are the true evidences of having passed from spiritual death, to the light and liberty of God's own children! And it is to the standard of pure religion, that the Church at this time endeavors to recall us. A perpetual witness for the faith, her voice is heard " through the ages all along, publishing truths of which an evil world would willingly lose sight, and pointing her members to the bright examples of those who, in earlier, purer days, " fought the good fight," and " inherited the promises." From her we learn, that religion consists, not in talking much and eloquently on the subject—not alone in striving to feel spiritually — not even in being warm and earnest in aiding the progress of the Church. An individual may do all these things, and yet be only like " sounding brass or a tinkling cymbal." That faith of the heart by which we " believe unto righteousness," is no wavering impulse. It is a fixed, steadfast habit of the mind, shown by our renouncing the spirit of the world — subduing our own evil tempers — living " soberly, righteously, and godly " — " crucifying the flesh, with the affections and lusts " — and acting in truth as the self-denying followers of that Master of whom it is recorded, that He " pleased not Himself."

And while the Church thus defines the evi·

dences of spiritual life, and declares the Christian
conflict to be " an earnest, endless strife,"[20] she at
the same time most sternly rebukes the compro-
mising spirit of the day. She summons her
children to come out from a sinful and apostate
world. She bids them not live as other men do,
in ease and idleness, when so much is to be accomplished for their Lord. She inquires how
they can be " delicate on the earth," when they
are called by their Master to " drink of the cup
of which He drank," and to be conformed to Him
alike in His sufferings and His life. And it is
by the abstinence and self-mortification of this
solemn season, that she strives to impress these
lessons. If therefore they listen to her teaching,
and tread this scene of mists and shadows beneath
their feet, each returning year will endow them
with added strength, while they travel onward
to that world of light, to which she points them
as their eternal home. They will learn to despise

---

[20] " One only way to life;
   One faith delivered once for all;
   One holy band, endowed with Heaven's high call;
   One earnest, endless strife—
   This is the Church th' Eternal framed of old."
                                        Lyra Apostolica.

the fleeting and the perishable, and even while still imprisoned in this tabernacle of clay their spirits will yearn for communion with the Enduring and the Infinite.

Another reason for the institution of this season in Primitive times was — WITH REFERENCE TO TWO CLASSES OF INDIVIDUALS WHO WERE THEN TO BE RECEIVED INTO THE CHURCH.

One class was that of the *Catechumens*, who had been preparing for Baptism. As Easter was the fixed and solemn time for their admission to this rite,[21] the Church fasted with them as a preparatory step to their commencing a religious life. Thus Justin Martyr in the second century declares — " As many as are persuaded, and do believe that the things taught and said by us are true, and promise to live accordingly, they are instructed to pray, and with fasting to beg of God remission of sins, we praying and fasting

---

[21] The most celebrated time for Baptism in the early Church, was *Easter;* next to that, *Pentecost,* or *Whitsuntide,* and then *Epiphany.* The Church however still allowed her members the liberty to anticipate these times, if either Catechumens were great proficients, or in danger of death by disease or any sudden accident. — BINGHAM'S *Orig. Eccles.,* lib. xi., ch. 6, sec. 7.

3

together with them. Then they are brought to
the place where water is, and are regenerated
after the same manner of regeneration as we
were regenerated before them."[22] In the same
manner, Cyril of Jerusalem thus addresses the
Catechumens: "The present season is a season
of confession; all worldly cares are to be laid
aside, for you strive for your souls. You that
have been busy about the things of the world,
and troubled in vain for many years, will ye not
bestow forty days in prayer for the salvation of
your souls?" And again, he says — "there is a
large time given you. You have the Penance
before you of forty days, sufficient space and
opportunity to put off the old garments and put
on the new."[23] Upon this account all candidates
for baptism were obliged to give in their names,
forty days before the administration of the rite.

Such was the interest the early Christians took
in those who were to be united with them in the
fellowship of the Church. They were jealous for
the honor of their Master, and the purity of the
faith. They were earnest that those about to

[22] BINGHAM, lib. xxi., ch. 1, sec. 12.
[23] BINGHAM, lib. xxi., ch. 1, sec. 12.

avow His name should not walk unworthy of
their calling, and therefore through all this season,
they prayed and fasted with them. They felt a
zeal for the whole body of the faithful, and an
ardent desire that no stain should rest upon the
religion they professed. They realized, that they
were a little band, surrounded by a world which
loved them not. Beyond their own little circle
they could expect no sympathy, but lived isolated
and apart from those among whom they dwelt.
When therefore, as was always done by the
Apostles, they were addressed as " brethren," a
chord was struck, which vibrated through every
heart. They knew that they were " heirs *together*
of the grace of life."

May we not therefore take " shame and confusion of face" to ourselves, because we are so
deficient in this feeling! In this age of cold and
selfish worldliness, we have almost ceased to
regard the " communion of Saints" as a reality.
And yet, though we think not of it, the tie is a
most holy one, which unites those who are disciples of the same faith. They are looking upward
to a common Master, invisible indeed to the
eye of sense, yet whose presence they every

where recognize in the occurrences of daily life.
Combatants in the same warfare, they are ex·
posed to equal dangers — are contending against
common enemies — share in the same hopes and
fears — and when the hour of victory comes, ex·
pect to join in one triumph, and rejoice in the
same bright reward. It is no imaginary bond,
therefore, which unites in fellowship the faithful
in Christ Jesus. It is a community of interest in
all that men should count most valuable. They
are members of one great fraternity, which
gathers out its chosen ones from every generation, and includes the just who have already
passed into the promised Canaan, and those who
are still toiling onward in the wilderness. In the
beautiful words of one of our own hymns—

> " Angels, and living saints, and dead,
>   But one communion make ;
> All join in Christ, their vital Head,
>   And of His love partake."

And the reason why this great truth is now
so little appreciated, is obvious. It is because
heresy and schism have entered " the consecrated
host of God's elect," rending it asunder, tearing
in pieces " the body of Christ, which is His

Church," and arraying the followers of the same
Lord against each other in hostile bands. Every
strange form of error which the intellect of fallen
man could engraft upon the Gospel, is rife around
us, until the pure Faith stands like Milton's personification of Chastity, amidst "the rout of
monsters" who composed the crew of Comus.
The Church herself is as a beleaguered city, and
the countless parties by which she is encircled,
"have pitched their tents all about the holy camp,
like the mixed multitude that followed the true
Israel of God from out the land of Egypt."
And the result is, that men become accustomed
to the sight of discord and the cry of disunion.
They even forget the "fellowship" which should
subsist between those who "continue steadfastly
in the Apostles' doctrine, and in breaking of
bread, and in prayers." Party names fill the
earth, and individuals withdraw themselves into
their own little circles, and send forth no sympathy and love to the millions who are without,
though their faith may be the same. But how
different is this from the feeling which prevailed
in ancient times! Then, when the fold of Christ
was one and her prayers in every place the

same, her members, wherever they were in the
earth, felt that they were among brethren, and
recognized in every lineament the same Church
which had existed "in their father's days, and in
the old time before them." Then, in the remote
East, and in Northern Africa, as well as in Western Europe, they were all united in "one Lord,
one faith, one baptism."

Touching indeed is the illustration given of this
truth, by the feelings awakened in the mind of a
celebrated Venetian traveler of those days, when
a wanderer from his home, in one of the cities of
distant England, he met a funeral train! "There
was nothing new, or strange, or singular, about
the burial procession, particularly calculated to
excite the attention of Marco Polo. The *De
Profundis* of the stoled priest spake the universal
language, adopted by the most sublime of human
compositions, the Liturgy of Western Christendom. Yet, though no objects appeared which
could awaken any lively curiosity in the traveler,
there was much in their familiarity to excite the
sympathy of the wanderer in a foreign land.
With an altered tone he said to the friar, ' Sad-
dened is the spirit of the pilgrim, by the dying

twilight and the plaining Vesper bell. But he who braves every danger for himself, may feel his heart sink within him when the pageant of triumphant death brings to his mind the thought, that those from whom as he weened, he parted for a little time only, may have been already borne to the sepulchre. Yet there is also a great and enduring comfort to the traveler in Christendom. However uncouth may be the speech of the races amongst whom the pilgrim sojourns, however diversified may be the customs of the regions which he visits, let him enter the portal of the Church, or hear, as I do now, the voice of the minister of the Gospel, and he is present with his own, though Alps and oceans may sever them asunder. There is one spot where the pilgrim always finds his home. We are all one people when we come before the Altar of the Lord.' "[24]

How beautiful is this picture! and how sad does it make the change which now we witness! What a dejection of spirit often comes over the Christian, as he is reminded of this subject in repeating the Confession — " I believe in one Catholic and Apostolic Church ! " Is there not

[24] Sir FRANCIS PALGRAVE'S *Merchant and Friar*, p. 138.

reason, then, at this Holy season, when the Universal Church is every where at the same time prostrating herself before the Lord, that we should pray for a return of those golden days when the faithful were one in heart and name? Yes — though oceans may roll between, and we never meet face to face on earth, we have still an interest in each one who is united with the Church, wherever he may be, for we are all " members of one another." Let us then petition our Common Father, that he will grant us more of that spirit which distinguished the Christian host in earlier and better days, until we realize, that He " has knit together his elect in one communion and fellowship, in the mystical body of His Son Christ our Lord."[25]

The other class of persons, who were preparing at this time to be received into the Church, were the *Penitents*, who had once been cut off for their sins, but after having completed their Canonical time of probation, during which they were excluded from her services, were generally absolved and readmitted at the time of the Easter Festival. Some of them for flagrant sins had

[25] Collect for All Saints' Day.

been kept under this penitential discipline for years, until by evident humility and earnestness, they had given the fullest proof of their contrition and amendment.[26] It is to this that an ancient Bishop refers, when he says—" The Anniversary solemnity of Easter, was not only the time of regenerating Catechumens, but of begetting those again to a lively hope, who had forfeited it by their sin, but were desirous to regain it by repentance and conversion from dead works, to walk again in the paths of life."[27] Cyprian also in his Epistles, speaks of Easter as the great and solemn time of readmitting Penitents.

These indeed were the days of rigid discipline

[26] The discipline was far from being nominal. It was often such as nothing but the deepest feelings of contrition could have induced them to bear. In some cases, they were obliged to appear in sackcloth, with ashes on their heads — the men to cut off their hair, and the women to go veiled, as a token of sorrow and mourning — to abstain from feasting, and even the innocent diversions of life — to practice abstinence, mortification and fasting, in private, as well as to observe the public fasts of the Church — to show their liberality to the poor in an eminent degree — and in some Churches to exercise their humility by taking upon themselves the office and care of burying the dead. See BINGHAM, lib. xviii., ch. 2, sec. 4.

[27] Gregory Nyssen. (BINGHAM, lib. xxi., ch. 1, sec. 13.)

3*

in the Church, when the offender was obliged
to make his confession and his repentance as
open as his sin, that no stain might rest upon the
purity of the faith. And in enforcing these rules,
no immunity was granted to rank or power.
Look, for example, at the case of the Emperor
Theodosius. Having ordered a massacre by his
troops at Thessalonica, in which several thousand
lives were sacrificed, St. Ambrose, the Bishop of
Milan, at once charged him with his guilt, and
refused to hold intercourse with one thus stained
with innocent blood. The doors of the Church
were closed against the Master of the world,
and he was commanded to bow to that authority
which is above all earthly rule. The subordina-
tion of the civil to the ecclesiastical power was
clearly proclaimed in that emphatic sentence —
" The Emperor is of the Church, and in the
Church, but not above the Church." Having
desired, even on the Festival of the Nativity, to
attend its services, he was met at the entrance of
the sanctuary by the intrepid prelate, who boldly
rebuked him for his want of humility, and ordered
him not to pollute the temple with his presence
until he had been absolved from his iniquity.

Thus, for eight months, he was ignominiously excluded from those holy offices of the Church which were freely afforded to the meanest of his subjects — even to the beggar and the slave. Theodosius pleaded in his defence the example of David. "Since then you have imitated his offence" — replied the Bishop — "imitate also his penitence." At length, on his public humiliation, St. Ambrose consented to admit the Emperor, not into the Church itself, but into the outer porch, the place for the public penitents. There, prostrate on the pavement, stripped of his imperial ornaments, beating his breast, and watering the ground with his tears, the master of the Roman Empire, and the legislator of the world, received his hard wrung absolution. Thus it was that the Church then stood forth as the champion of the oppressed, and extended her penalties over the mightiest of the earth.[28]

But how imposing must have been this penitential discipline, so rigorously enforced! "The Church was not then divided into separate independent bodies, holding no communication with

---

[28] MILMAN's *History of Christianity*, vol. ii., p. 230.

each other, which might enable an offender when expelled from one to attach himself to another, ' and thus maintain, in defiance of his condemners, an outward union with Christ. He might as well have endeavored to escape the penalties of rebellion against the head of the Roman Empire by removing from one province to another. So spotless too was her innocence, so bright her holiness, that none dared question for a moment the justice of her decisions; and her sentence, however rigorous it might be, was deemed to be ratified in Heaven; to be cut off from her, was effectually to be cut off from Christ. Thus, both her blessings and her censures were an outward expression, an earthly type, by which men were warned of what judgment was proceeding in Heaven upon their conduct of life, and her slowness of forgiveness, and the fiery probation to which she submitted the penitent, were well calculated to dispel those hurtful notions which men now so generally entertain of the ease and the speed of the process of forgiveness of sins."[29] The multitude, often but partially reclaimed from

[29] *Rectory of Valehead*, p. 164.

barbarism, who could be restrained by no worldly
motives, and over whom the civil authority of the
land exerted but little power when it came into
conflict with their passions, were obliged to trem-
ble as the awful denunciations of the Church fell
upon their ears. To them there was a fearful yet
salutary lesson taught, by the public shame of the
penitent — his deep humiliation — the bitterness
and intensity of his remorse. It was with these
individuals, then, whose probation had been so
severe, but who were now again to be received
into the body of the faithful, that the Church at
this season prayed and fasted, that their sins
might be washed away, and the comfortable
hope which once they had forfeited be again
restored.

And if the evil days on which we have fallen,
prevent the Church in this age from enforcing
with a wholesome severity, her primitive discipline, is there not double reason why her members should bewail their sins, and pray God not
to visit upon them the recompense of their
offences? Should not their petition be—" Spare
thy people, good Lord, and let not thine heritage
be brought to confusion?" And in harmony

with such convictions, we find that all the ser
vices of Lent breathe an evident feeling of contrition — that we every where present ourselves
n the attitude of humility, and pray our merciful
Father to grant us " perfect remission and forgiveness." Let us strive then to partake of the
spirit of these petitions: and when we look around
us and remember how far, as a Church, we have
wandered from the path of primitive holiness,
how lukewarm is our devotion, and how feeble
our faith compared with what it should be, we
shall realize that there is reason for that deep
and searching penitence which our Master seeks
to kindle up within us, and the expression of
which is heard so often in our Liturgy.

These, then, are the reasons which induced
the early Church to institute this Holy Season,
thus exercising the power entrusted to her, " to
decree rites and ceremonies."[80] It is with her
sanction that we are summoned to its observance.
It is impressed upon us by the solemn voice
which comes down from the years of a distant
and dim antiquity. In these services many gen-

[80] Article xx. *Of the Authority of the Church*—"The
Church hath power to decree rites or ceremonies."

erations have already joined, and thus gathered
strength for the journey which lay before them.
They have long since passed away, leaving to us
not only their bright examples, but also the
record of their experience. We stand in their
places. We are the honored guardians of all
those rites and institutions which they in their
day found useful in the Church, and then bequeathed to such as should come after them.
Solemn indeed is the trust — may we never betray it! May we always remember that we are
" baptized for the dead" — inheriting their re-
sponsibilities — enjoying the fruits of their labors
— and that we must commit this sacred heritage
undiminished to our successors. Let us never
then be willing to give up these ancient services,
which were used by the holy dead, whose memory we love, or to substitute in their place the
novelties of an age " emulous of change." Let
us be content to tread the path which still gleams
brightly with the steps of those who for Christ's
sake and the gospel's " counted not their lives
dear unto themselves." Let us strive, as they
did, against an unholy world—loving with a true
devotion, the Church for which they died — and

seeking to imbibe the spirit which reigns in her courts. And then, when "life's fitful fever" is over, we shall be admitted with the just whom we have followed on earth, to the Paradise of God — to "the general assembly and Church of the first-born, which are written in Heaven."

THE PROPER OBSERVANCE OF LENT.

Nor wonder that the widow'd Church should sound
  Of sadness; there are mourners CHRIST hath blest,
Who watch with her their annual, weekly round,
  And in obedience fir d the promis'd rest.

The Cathedral.

II.

THE PROPER OBSERVANCE OF LENT.

We are told, that in one of the darkest periods of Jerusalem's apostacy, and when her ruin by a powerful invader was just at hand, another reprieve was granted, and one more summons to repentance sent forth. "And in that day did the Lord God of Hosts call to weeping, and to mourning, and to baldness, and to girding with sackcloth; and behold, joy and gladness." Thus it was, that her people scorned the prophet's message, and turned as usual to their worldly pleasures. But the decision of God upon their conduct, is thus given by Isaiah: "And it was revealed in mine ear by the Lord of Hosts, Surely this iniquity shall not be purged from you till ye die, saith the Lord God of Hosts."[1]

[1] Isaiah xxii., 12, 13, 14.

And thus, by the voice of His Church, is God
at this season calling us also " to weeping and
mourning." So comprehensive too is the summons, that none who bear the Christian name can
plead exemption. The command is — Blow the
trumpet in Zion, sanctify a fast, call a solemn
assembly, gather the people, sanctify the congre-
gation, assemble the elders, gather the children,
and those that suck at the breasts; let the bridegroom go forth of his chamber, and the bride out
of her closet; let the priests, the ministers of the
Lord, weep between the porch and the altar, and
let them say, Spare thy people, O Lord, and give
not thy heritage to reproach.[2]   In this way it is,
we are directed, by chastening our spirits, to prepare to celebrate our Lord's solemn sacrifice —
that mysterious passion and agony which the
world can never fully comprehend, and to the
history of which it can only listen, with an awful
reverence. How then shall we keep this holy
season? How can we most fully enter into the
spirit of its services—availing ourselves of these
opportunities to approach our God—afflicting the

[2] Scripture appointed for the Epistle for Ash-Wednesday.

soul now, that hereafter it may be saved forever? In answer to these inquiries, and that we may know how to carry out the design of the Church for our spiritual benefit, let us look at some of the methods in which we may best observe this solemn period of our Ecclesiastical year.

ABSTINENCE FROM WORLDLY AMUSEMENTS, is one particular which most naturally occurs to us. In the early Church, not only was the attendance of her members on all public games and shows forbidden during the season of Lent, but the prohibition was even extended to the celebration of marriages, and the anniversaries of birth days, because these took place with feasting, and tokens of joy and pleasure, inappropriate to a season which should be devoted to deep humiliation and mourning.[3] St. Chrysostom, in his Lent sermons, inveighs with his usual zeal, against any violation of these salutary rules. In the midst of his sharp invectives against those who had attended the Circus at this time, he says: "When I consider, how at one blast of the devil ye have forgotten all my daily admonitions and continued discourses, and run to that pomp of Satan, the horse-race in

[3] See BINGHAM'S *Orig. Eccles.*, lib. xxi., ch. 1, sec. 21.

the Circus, with what heart can I think of preaching to you again, who have so soon let slip all
that I said before? This is what chiefly raises
my grief, yea my anger and indignation, that
together with my admonition ye have cast the
reverence of this holy season of Lent out of your
souls, and thrown yourselves into the nets of the
devil. What profit is there in your fasting!
What advantage in your meeting together so
often in this place?"[4] And again, in another
Homily, while in a pathetic manner exhibiting
to them the moral influence of this conduct, his
language is—"Subdue, I beseech you, this wicked
and pernicious custom. And consider, that they
who run to the Circus, not only do much harm
to themselves, but are the occasion of great scandal to others. For when the Jews and Gentiles
see you, who are every day at Church to hear a
sermon, come notwithstanding to the horse-race,
and join with them in the Circus, will they not
reckon our religion a cheat, and entertain the
same suspicion of us all? They will sharpen their
tongues against us all, and for the offences of a
few condemn the whole body of Christians.

[4] St. Chrys., tom. ii., p. 49, Hom. 6, in Gen.

Neither will they stop here, but rail at our Head, and for the servant's fault blaspheme our common Lord, and think that a sufficient apology and excuse for their own errors, that they have something to object to the life and conversation of others."[5]

And if worldly amusements have in this age changed their form, still their nature and influence are the same. A ceaseless struggle for our affections is going on, and the choice we make determines our state, not only in this life, but through all the wasteless ages of our immortality. The tempter still arrays before the Christian, the glare and gaudiness of this fleeting scene, that his attention may be distracted, and his progress towards Heaven impeded. On the other hand, it is the object of our faith, to cause him to look away beyond " things seen and temporal " to those which are " unseen and eternal." We must live in this lower world, as pilgrims whose hopes and affections are not here—who bear about with them the consciousness that this is not their home, but that they are only journeyers through the wilderness, toiling onward to the promised land.

[5] St. Chrys., tom. ii., p. 61, Hom. 7, in Gen.

We are to be like St. Paul, " crucified with our
Lord to the world, and the world to us "—gazing
on its pleasures with the same unconcern with
which the dying man would from the Cross—
putting it from us, and leaving untried no means
which may avail, to destroy the witchery of its
enchantments, and to break its power over our
hearts.   We are even to give up its lawful comforts and its innocent enjoyments, when called to
this sacrifice for any worthy end; for there may
come occasion to the follower of the Lord to
" take pleasure in infirmities, in reproaches, in
necessities, in persecutions, in distresses for Christ's
sake."   Thus, in striving to be more conformed
to his Master, or more entirely to be disentangled
from this scene of temptation, he may be obliged
to offer upon the altar of Christian duty, all those
affections which twine most closely about the
heart, " losing his life for Christ's sake and the
Gospel's, that he may save it."

> " Sweet is the smile of home ; the mutual look
>   When hearts are of each other sure ;
> Sweet all the joys that crowd the household nook,
>   The haunt of all affections pure ;
> Yet in the world even these abide, and we
>   Above the world our calling boast :

Once gain the mountain top, and thou art free;
Till then, who rest, presume; who turn to look, are
lost." [6]

It was to escape the unholy influence of this
world's fascinations, that the followers of our
Lord were accustomed, in the olden time, to flee
from this scene of trial, and in the solitary her-
mitage, or the desert waste, where no man was,
to pass their lives in communion with their God,
and in making ready for their last account. But
no precept of Scripture authorized them to rend
the ties of duty, and for a selfish motive, to burst
the chains which bound them to home and kindred. "It is a wretched righteousness"—says
Luther, in one of his letters to Spenlein—"which
will not bear with others, because it deems them
evil, and seeks the solitude of the desert, instead
of doing good to such, by long suffering, by
prayer, and example. If thou art the lily and
the rose of Christ, know that thy dwelling-place
is among thorns."

Nor did they by this desertion attain their
object. The piety at which they aimed, was
tinged with dreamy reveries, and evaporated in

[6] KEBLE's *Christian Year.* First Sunday in Lent.

4

contemplation of an imaginary purity. The passions in their breasts which they had hoped to
root out, turned inward, and centered in themselves, and they found that if they could escape
from the world without, they must still carry
with them that little world within, in subduing
which the conflict chiefly consists. They had
cast from them the weapons of their warfare, and
fled from the strife, leaving an ungodly world to
roll on to destruction, unrebuked and unaided,
and they reaped their retribution. They deprived
themselves of all those' high and ennobling feelings, which purify the heart, while they animate
men to exertion. Their selfishness recoiled upon
themselves, and the dreamy enthusiast who wished
to be wiser than Scripture, and to improve upon
the example of his Lord, found that he had not
added to the fortitude of his virtue. He had
sacrificed his happiness, and become but too often
only a gloomy misanthrope.[7]

[7] These remarks will of course apply only to the solita-
ries. While their cells were the very nurseries of superstition, they were said, in the language of Alcuin, "to lead
an angelical life." Archbishop Leighton, however, much
more truly describes an angelical life, as " a life spent between ascending in prayer to fetch blessings from above,

The true trial of our life here is to meet with
evil, and yet by God's grace to overcome it —
to be *in* the world, and yet so to trample it under
our feet as to show, that we are not *of* the

and descending to scatter them among men." The monastic institutions were free from many of those difficulties of
which we have spoken, and in the purer days of the Church
rendered essential service to the cause of religion, when
society around was in a rude and almost barbarous state.
The monks were often learned and industrious — the pat-
terns of active virtue — the liberal dispensers of charity —
and the zealous promoters of learning and the useful arts.
" It was a great benefit, that there should be places of
education, where the young might be trained for the service of the Church or State: it was well that there should
be places of retirement where the aged might end their
days in penitence and prayer; and places of refuge, where
the orphan and friendless might find support and protec-
tion." (CHURTON's *Early Eng. Church*, p. 104. See chap.
v, vi.) They who in the reign of Henry VIII. were grasp-
ing at the wealth of monasteries, eagerly united to villify
their occupants, and succeeding generations have quietly
received their report, with scarcely the trouble of a doubt.
But the true history of the monastic institution is yet to
be written, by one, who with a philosophical eye can read
its influence on the spirit of the age and the character of
society, and who is ready with an unprejudiced, impartial
feeling to acknowledge its benefits, while he points out the
evils to which it ultimately gave birth.

It is probably not known to many of our readers, that there
are in the kingdom of Hanover, eleven Protestant convents,
or (to give them a better name) " religious houses." They

world — to have its fascinations around us, and yet to turn from them. Its Circean song may float sweetly to our ears, but yet it must not beguile us to pass over into the land of its enchantments. It is in the fiery ordeal of temptation, and amidst the din and struggle of the conflict, that man learns to know himself, and to estimate aright his own spiritual powers. His hopes become more clear after every conquest which he makes—his reliance upon things unseen and eternal is strengthened—and his whole Christian character is matured and perfected. " This is the victory that overcometh the world, even our faith." There is true wisdom indeed in the eloquent words of Milton, when he says — " He that can apprehend and consider vice with all her baits and seeming pleasures, and yet abstain, and yet distinguish, and yet prefer that which is

are asylums, to which respectable females " when thrown out upon the world by the dissolution of their families, can retire, without experiencing those mortifications which are so frequently attendant upon adversity." (Dwight's *Germany*, p. 100.) An English lady has of late years founded a similar house, at Clifton, near Bristol (Churton's *Early Eng. Church*, p. 382.) The inmates of none of these institutions, however, are bound by those ensnaring vows which produced much of the evil in the Romish Church.

truly better, he is the true wayfaring Christian.
I cannot praise a fugitive and cloistered virtue,
unexercised and unbreathed, that never sallies
out and sees her adversary, but slinks out of the
race, where that immortal garland is to be run
for, not without dust and heat. That which puri-
fies us is trial, and trial is by what is contrary.
Which was the reason why our sage and serious
poet Spencer, describing true Temperance under
the person of Guion, brings him in with his
Palmer through the cave of Mammon, and the
bower of earthly bliss, that he might see and
know, and yet abstain."

Yet it is evident, on the other hand, that a
temporary retirement from the bustle and tumult
of this busy life, is requisite to enable the spirit
to shake off the worldliness which has been insensibly growing upon it, and to plume its wings
again for Heaven. It is necessary, that man
should now and then withdraw within himself,
think of his eternal interests, and examine with
peculiar care, his account with God. " We must
retire inward " — says St. Bernard, — " if we
would ascend upward." It is with this view,
therefore, that the Church from the earliest age,

has yearly in the season of Lent, recalled her
children from the absorbing cares of time, and
gathered them into her own bosom, to meditate
and pray.

The question — how much under ordinary circumstances, we may mingle in the gayeties and
amusements of the world — is one which each
individual must determine for himself. He knows
their effect upon his own heart, and the influence
of his example upon those around him, and must
act accordingly. If after having in baptism
solemnly renounced " the pomps and vanities of
this wicked world," he still thinks it right to devote himself to them, he must be guided by his
own conscience in this important decision. If
he thinks it fit, that on Sunday his friends should
see him kneeling at the altar, professing to forsake the world, and then on the week day, meet
him in all its frivolities and gayeties, until they
suspect that his religion is only intended to be
put on in Church, his is the responsibility, and
his must be the retribution. To his own Master
he must stand or fall. But the hour is rapidly
coming, when from the bed of death and the bar
of judgment, each one will be forced to look back

upon these scenes, and decide whether he acted well and wisely while life was going on.[8]

Yet there are times and seasons, when there can be no mistake on this subject, and when the

[8] One of the most common charges against the Church is, that her members are permitted to mingle in the gayeties of the world in a manner inconsistent with the Christian character, and particularly to frequent theatrical amusements. This is no place, of course, to discuss the question, whether they do so more than those who are connected with the different denominations around them. We can only say, that when Churchmen are found in this situation — thus bringing discredit on their profession — it is in utter violation of the rules of the Church, and at variance with the spirit she endeavors to inculcate upon them by every one of her services, from the comprehensive Baptismal Vow, even to that last solemn prayer in the Visitation of the Sick, which commends the departing soul to the mercy of its God. As conclusive evidence of the sense of the Church on this point, we can give the highest authority — that of the House of Bishops in General Convention. It stands thus recorded on their Journal:

" *Tuesday, May* 27*th*, 1817. Resolved, That the following be entered on the Journal of this House and be sent to the House of Clerical and Lay Deputies, to be read therein:

" The House of Bishops, solicitous for the preservation of the purity of the Church, and the piety of its members, are induced to impress upon the Clergy the important duty, with a discreet but earnest zeal, of warning the people of their respective cures, of the danger of an indul

Church has decided that her children must retire, in a peculiar manner, from this world, to think of that which is to come. Such, for instance, is the week which precedes the administration of the Holy Communion. It is with reference to this, that her ministers are commanded, " to give

gence in those worldly pleasures which may tend to withdraw the affections from spiritual things. And especially on the subject of gaming, of amusements involving cruelty to the brute creation, *and of theatrical representations*, to which some peculiar circumstances have called their attention — they do not hesitate to express their unanimous opinion, *that these amusements, as well from their licentious tendency, as from the strong temptations to vice which they afford, ought not to be frequented.* And the Bishops can not refrain from expressing their deep regret at the information that in some of our large cities so little respect is paid to the feelings of the members of the Church, that theatrical representations are fixed for the evenings of her most solemn Festivals."—*Jour. of Gen. Con.* 1817, page 46.

Any one acquainted with the regular steps of degradation through which the theatre has passed during the last twenty-five years, will acknowledge that if it had "a licentious tendency" in 1817, that demoralizing influence is doubly powerful in this day. Let not then occasional inconsistencies of members of the Church — inconsistencies, we believe, becoming each year more rare — be brought forward as any illustration of the spirit of the Church. These are the exceptions, and their conduct is looked upon by their fellow members with sorrow and shame.

warning for its celebration upon the Sunday or some holy day immediately preceding." And at the same time it is made their duty to their hearers, " to exhort them in the mean season, so to search and examine their own consciences, that they may come holy and clean to such a heavenly feast, in the marriage garment required by God in Holy Scripture, and be received as worthy partakers of that holy table." Now unless this appeal is a mere formality, and means nothing, surely we are expected in the interval to prepare ourselves for uniting in that solemn mystery, and no one needs this preparation more than the individual who loves this world so well that he finds it hard to obey the injunction. But is this to be done, amidst the bustle and excitement of worldly pleasure? No — it is not there that God is accustomed to meet us, with the influences of His grace, or the rich aids of His Spirit. Let us not then endeavor, thus to mingle earth with Heaven, or to come to our Master's solemn feast with thoughts distracted by frivolity and amusement. Let us walk entirely as " children of the light," or not attempt to worship at the altars both of Christ and Belial.

4*

Such a season, again, is that of Lent. Listen
to the tones of earnest repentance which the services of the Church breathe forth, and then say,
whether after giving utterance to these, we can
rush at once into the embraces of a world, from
which we have just prayed to be delivered. But
are there any, who feel that six weeks is too long
a time to withdraw from earthly pleasures?
What — we would ask in reply — what must be
the state of that spirit—what its preparation for
Heaven — in which such thoughts could be entertained? This cleaving to the objects of our
earthly worship — this miserable hankering after
pleasures we profess to have abandoned — proclaim but too clearly a self-deceived heart, still
unbaptized by the Spirit from on high. Such an
one has reason to fear, lest the day of solemn
trial find him without the wedding garment.
When at this season then, God calls to " weeping
and mourning," shall it be said of us, " behold,
joy and gladness ? "

SELF-EXAMINATION is another obvious duty
which we must perform during the period of
Lent. This naturally follows from what has
been already advanced. If we withdraw from

the world, it is not that we may spend our
time in listless idleness, but that we may employ
ourselves in girding up our loins anew, and trim-
ming our lamps, to be ready for our Lord's
appearing. It is that we may "commune with
our own hearts and be still." It is, that we
may review the past, and as we compare our
actions with the law of God, decide whether or
not we are walking in the way of His command-
ments.

And who that knows the deceitfulness of the
human heart — who that has ever read our Master's repeated warnings that we should "watch"
— will say that this is unnecessary! We go
forth to the world, with our decision made to
serve the Lord, and our Christian hopes burning
brightly; but as one day after another passes by,
insensibly we lose the simplicity of our religious
character, and become at last "of the earth
earthly," before we even suspect that we have
departed from the fervor of our earliest love.
"The gold becomes dim, and the fine gold
changed." Our thoughts are drawn off from
our Master and his cause, until the excitements
and allurements which are around produce their

natural result, and we begin to be willing to take our portion with those whom we had professed to leave. We learn to persuade ourselves, to yield in things which a more tender conscience would have taught us to refuse, until our service becomes partial and worldly, and we are no longer heartily devoted to the Lord.

Now, how many thus pass through life? At times, the monitor within utters its voice, and they are forced to doubt, whether or not they are in the faith. Yet they at once dispel these disagreeable thoughts. From a natural indolence of disposition, they shrink from the task of investigating their own hearts. They seem willing to live along, trusting that it may in the end be well with them. They postpone to the last day, the decision of the most solemn question this world can furnish, although then it will be too late to rectify an error. Is it not therefore well for us, at times to stop in our worldly career, and settle this point? Many are the lessons of solemn caution which our Master gave, to guard against this very danger. The rich man who thought not of death — the servants who ate and drank, but remembered not their Lord's return — and the virgins who slept when the bridegroom was at hand, and then awoke only to bitter disappointment — are all set forth for our warning. And how miserable would be our state, should the summons thus be heard when we expect it not, and then for the first time the full consciousness burst upon us, that we have been deceiving our own hearts, and serving the world! Let us therefore watch and examine ourselves, that as time passes by, there may grow no rust upon our souls, and no habitual sin darken the mirror on which the pure light of Heaven should be reflected. Let us not, when once we have girded on our armor, lay it aside or be found sleeping at our post. In the solemn day of our Master's appearing, when " all kindreds of the earth wail because of Him," let us be found among those chosen ones, whom the Church has gathered into her fold, trained in every holy work, and purified for her Lord, that they might be found ready when His marriage hour should come.

There is one more way, by which we should peculiarly mark this season as one of penitence— it is by FASTING. On the morning of Ash-Wed-

nesday, we prostrate ourselves before our God
and say — " Be favorable, O Lord, be favorable
to thy people, who turn to Thee in weeping.
fasting and praying." And yet by how many,
have we not reason to fear, are these words
uttered, who shrink from the Christian duty of
which they speak! It is much more easy to
offer unto God the tribute of our lips, than to
chasten and discipline the body. We believe it
is for this reason, that in these days when men
seek their own comfort, this practice which has
prevailed through all ages of the Jewish and
Christian Churches, has fallen so much into
disuse.

Yet take up the word of God, and what duty
is spoken of more decidedly, or the performance
of which is more frequently followed by a blessing! Joshua and the elders of Israel, when de-
feated by the men of Ai, kept a solemn fast, as
they remained all day, " until the even-tide,"
prostrate on the earth before the ark, with dust
upon their heads, in humiliation and prayer.
And the result was, that victory again attended
them. David fasted as well as prayed, when he
humbled himself before God after his sin against

Uriah, and although deprived of his child, yet his iniquity was forgiven. The inhabitants of Nineveh, in fear of judgments obeyed the decree of their King, when he proclaimed — " Let neither man nor beast, herd nor flock, taste any thing; let them not feed nor drink water; but let man and beast be covered with sackcloth, and cry mightily unto God "—and their city was spared. The devoted Ezra, when setting out for Jerusalem, assembled the returning captives at the river Ahava, and there " proclaimed a fast, that they might afflict themselves before God, and seek of Him a right way for themselves and their little ones, and for all their substance " — and he obtained the blessing he asked. And thus we might go through the Old Testament, and show that on every important occasion, the ancient saints under the former dispensation not only prayed but fasted also.

And so it continued to be, when the Gospel dawned upon the earth. *Anna was " serving God with fastings and prayers, night and day," when her petition was answered, and she saw her Saviour. Our Lord himself, before he entered on His public ministry, passed through a long period of preparatory fasting. The Apostles did so, before every solemn act in which they engaged. They were " in fastings often." St. Paul frequently refers to the use of this means of grace. He declares, that he " approves himself a minister of God," as in other things, so " in fastings also ;" and he writes to the Corinthians — " Give yourselves to fasting and prayer." Cornelius, " the devout centurion," was engaged in fasting, when the angel announced to him, that his alms and prayers had " come up for a memorial before God." St. Peter was fasting, when that wonderful vision revealed to him the admission of the Gentiles into the Church of God, and commissioned him to be to them, the earliest herald of the Gospel. The Church at Antioch was fasting, when the Holy Ghost said, " separate me Barnabas and Saul."

Neither can it be argued, that this was not expressly commanded by our Lord. He found the practice in use, and spake of it as one which should be continued. He gave directions to His disciples, how they ought to fast, and promised that they should be recompensed for the right performance of this duty. " But thou, when thou fastest, anoint thine head, and wash thy face; that thou appear not unto men to fast, but unto thy Father which is in secret; and thy Father which seeth in secret shall reward thee openly." Well therefore has Hooker remarked — " Our Lord and Saviour would not teach the manner of doing, much less propose a reward for doing, that which were not both holy and acceptable in God's sight."[9] But our Master also expressly declared, that after His departure His children in sorrow for his absence, should thus afflict themselves. " The days will come, when the bridegroom shall be taken from them, and then shall they fast." Does not this clearly prove the truth, that He considered it as a duty ?

What again, we would ask, means that declaration of His, with respect to the faith which could remove mountains ? " Howbeit this kind goeth not out, but by prayer and fasting." Do not these words imply, that there are nobler attainments in the Christian life to be gained by those, who through severity to themselves are able to strive after them? And do they not point out, " the unseen strength" of fasting as

9 *Eccles. Polity*, b. v., sec. 72.

that which is to enable the Christian warrior to
win the brightest crown? Yes, this is that
" more excellent way " which is opened to those
" who will receive it."

And this was the light in which the early
Church regarded this duty. In those days, when
they stood near to their Lord, and walked in
His hallowed footsteps, how often is this practice
mentioned as one, whose value the Church fully
appreciated! Thus St. Chrysostom says: —
" Though at other times when we preachers cry
up and preach the duty of fasting never so much
all the year, scarce any one hearkens to what we
say, yet when the season of forty days is come,
though none exhort or advise them, the most
negligent set themselves to it, taking admonition
and advice from the very season.[10] And again
he adds—" If a Jew or a Heathen ask you, why
do you fast? Do not tell him, it is for our
Saviour's Passion on the cross; for so you will
give him an handle to accuse you. For we do
not fast for the Passion or the Cross, but for our
sins, because we are come to the Holy Mysteries.
The Passion is not the occasion of fasting or

10 St. CHRYS., tom. v., Hom. 52, p. 709.

mourning, but of joy and exultation. We mourn not for that, but for our sins, and therefore we fast."

The manner too of their fasting in those ancient days, shows how thoroughly they desired to fulfill this duty. Instead of considering a change of food only as being sufficient, they entirely abstained from all sustenance through the whole day until the evening. Thus we find St. Ambrose, in one of his exhortations to his hearers to observe the Lent Fast, bidding them—"defer eating a little, because the end of the day is not far off."[11] St. Chrysostom in his Lent sermons frequently alludes to the same circumstance. " Let us " — he says — " set a guard upon our ears, our tongues, and minds, and not think that bare fasting till the evening is sufficient for our salvation."[12] And again in another passage, which we cannot forbear quoting entire, on account of the admirable view which it gives of this whole duty.

" The true fast is abstinence from vices. For abstinence from meat was appointed upon this

[11] Bing. *Orig. Eccles.*, lib. xxi., chap. 1, sec. 16.
[12] St. Chrys., tom ii., Hom. 4, in Gen., p. 37.

occasion, that we should curb the tone of our
flesh, and make the horse obedient to his rider.
He that fasts, ought above all things to bridle
his anger, and learn meekness and clemency, to
have a contrite heart, to banish the thoughts of
all inordinate desires, to set the watchful eye of
God before his eyes, and his uncorrupted judgment; to set himself above riches, and exercise
great liberality in giving of alms, and to expel
every evil thought against his neighbor out of
his soul. This is the true fast. Therefore let
this be our care, and let us not imagine, as many
do, that we have fasted rightly, when we have
abstained from eating until evening. This is not
the thing required of us, but that together with
our abstinence from meat, we should abstain
from those things that hurt the soul, and diligently exercise ourselves in things of a spiritual
nature."[18]

Yet we must not forget, in considering their
manner of fasting, that an Asiatic climate rendered comparatively easy what to us would appear to be an excessive severity. The lassitude
of constitution, and languor of the whole system,

<hr/>

[18] St. Chrys., Hom. 8, in Gen., p. 79.

which were produced by that genial temperature, enabled them to carry it to an extent, which in this latitude, or among the nations of Northern Europe, would be oppressive, and totally defeat the object for which it was undertaken.

Even in that day, however, this duty was per-formed with great allowance to human infirmi-ties; thus showing plainly, that instead of being made a superstitious form, it was used with refer-ence to its spiritual benefits. " Let no one "— says St. Chrysostom — " place his confidence in fasting only, if he continue in his sins without reforming. For it may be, one that fasts not at all, may obtain pardon, if he has the excuse of bodily infirmity. But he that does not correct his sins, can have no excuse. Thou hast not fasted by reason of the weakness of thy body; but why art thou not reconciled to thy enemies? Canst thou pretend bodily infirmity here? If thou retainest hatred and envy, what apology canst thou make? In such crimes as these thou canst not fly to the refuge of bodily weakness."[14] And again, in another Homily, he dwells upon this subject still more fully. " If thou canst not

[14] ST. CHRYS., Hom. 22, de Ira, tom. i., p. 277.

pass all the day fasting, by reason of bodily
weakness, no wise man can condemn thee for
this. For we have a kind and merciful Lord,
who requires nothing of us above our strength.
He neither requires abstinence from meat, nor
fasting simply of us, nor that for this end we
should continue without eating only; but that
withdrawing ourselves from worldly affairs, we
should pass all our leisure time in spiritual things.
For if we would order our lives soberly, and lay
out our spare hours upon spiritual things, and
eat only so much as we had need of, and nature
required, and spend our whole lives in good
works, we should not need the help of fasting.
But because human nature is negligent, and
gives itself rather ease and pleasure, therefore
our kind Lord, as a compassionate Father, hath
found out this medicine of fasting for us, that we
should abridge ourselves in our pleasures, and
transfer our care of secular things to works of a
spiritual nature. If therefore there be any here
present who are hindered by bodily infirmity,
and cannot continue all day fasting, I exhort
them to have regard to the weakness of their
bodies, and not upon that account deprive them

selves of spiritual instruction, but for that very
reason to pay more diligent attendance on it.
For there are many ways besides abstinence
from meat, which will open to us the door of confidence towards God. He therefore that eats,
and cannot fast, let him give the more plentiful
alms, let him be more fervent in his prayers, let
him show the greater alacrity and readiness in
hearing the divine oracles. For the weakness
of the body is no impediment in such offices as
these. Let him be reconciled to his enemies, and
forget injuries, and cast all thoughts of revenge
out of his mind. He that does these things, will
show forth the true fasting, which the Lord
chiefly requires. Therefore I exhort you who
are able to fast, to go on with all possible alacrity
in this good and laudable work, for by how much
more our outward man perishes, so much more
our inward man is renewed."[15]

And the same rule of moderation continues to
be that of the Church in our day. Caring for
the bodily as well as the spiritual health of her
members, she prescribes only such a degree of
fasting, as may keep our lower nature in subjec-

[15] St. Chrys., Hom. 10, in Gen., tom. ii., p. 91.

tion to that which is spiritual. Thus we are taught to pray on the first Sunday in Lent — " O Lord, who for our sake didst fast forty days and forty nights; give us grace to use such abstinence, that our flesh being subdued to the Spirit, we may ever obey Thy godly motions in righteousness and true holiness, to Thy honor and glory."

We would also observe, that united with this fast, or rather flowing from it, were more abundant deeds of charity. What they saved by their abstinence they expended on the poor. Thus, we find an Apostolic Father saying: — " A true fast is not merely to keep under the body, but to give to the widow or the poor, the amount of that which thou wouldst have expended upon thyself; that so he who receives it may pray to God for thee."[16]   Origen says — " He found it in some book as a noted saying of the Apostles, " Blessed is he who fasts for this end, that he may feed the poor; this man's fast is acceptable unto God."[17]   St. Chrysostom, in the extracts already given, alludes to this duty, and at a later

---

[16] *Hermas Pastor*, in COTEL., tom. i., p. 106.
[17] BING. *Orig. Eccles.*, lib. xxi., ch. 1, sec. 18.

period, we find St. Augustine writing—" Fasting
without almsgiving, is a lamp without oil."

Such then is the argument for this practice,
drawn from Scripture, and also the manner of
its performance in the early Church. It may be
thought by some, that too great a space has been
devoted to this discussion; but we must remember, that in the present day, there is probably no
duty so little understood, and so lightly evaded.
" We will practice mortification and self-denial
for learning's sake, but not for Christ's. We will
abstain from joys, and pleasures, and company,
and numberless indulgences, and put restraint
even on our loves, when ambition calls, but not
at the bidding of the Church. We will neglect
our health and rest, and become worn and pale,
and weary and weak, to gain earthly wisdom,
and power of intellect, and shorten our lives to
leave our names among posterity lifted some very
little, it may be, above the obscurity of the unnumbered dead. But to smooth down the severity of discipline, to have an easy Lent, or go
softly through a fast, we are ready to talk of our
health and habits, and way of living, and the
hardness of our duty, and the weakness of our

5

flesh, and in a light way of the mercy of our God. We are strong to do all things for ourselves, our own ambition strengthening us. We are weak for Christ, even though He be ready to give us strength."[18] And it is, we believe, because this duty is so little practised as a regu lar habit, that its benefits are so undervalued. It is often eagerly commenced in a fit of transient zeal, but the natural inclinations raise their remonstrance—it is found wearisome and painful — and after one or two attempts entirely laid aside. But is it not true, that this is scarcely giving it a trial? To be appreciated, and its benefits felt, it must be a habit — be practised often — and become, as it were, a portion of our regular religious service. Thus, that which at first was performed with difficulty, is rendered easy;[19] and we learn at last, that the ancient

[18] FABER's tracts on the *Offices of the Church.*

[19] GOETHE somewhere makes a remark, which may be applied to the whole circle of our religious duties: " Neither in moral or religious, more than in physical and civil matters, do people willingly do any thing suddenly or upon the instant; they need a succession of the like actions, whereby a habit may be formed; the things which they are to love, or to perform, they cannot conceive as insulated and detached; *whatever we are to repeat with satisfaction, must not have become foreign to us.*"

saints in Primitive days, knew human nature better than we do, and when they urged those who should come after them, to "crucify the flesh" as a source of spiritual benefits, were only giving the result of their own experience.

This then is that discipline, by whose severity we are to weaken the force of passion, and of those appetites which else assert the mastery over the soul, and bind it down to earth. " I keep under my body"—says St. Paul—" and bring it into subjection: lest that by any means when I have preached to others, I myself should be a cast away." And St. Chrysostom declares —" Fasting restrains the body, and checks and bridles its inordinate sallies, but makes the soul much lighter, and gives it wings to mount up and soar on high."[20] It teaches too, the habit of self-denial—leading us at intervals to remember that our object in this life is not to please ourselves, but rather to overcome temptation — to restrain and mortify the cravings of appetite. Thus we conquer that self-indulgence, which if permitted unfits us for spiritual duties.[21] And

---

[20] St. Chrys. Hom. 10, in Gen., tom. ii, p. 91.

[21] " It is a most miserable state for a man to have every

how forcibly also does it cause us to realize
things unseen and eternal! It is an act so contrary to the spirit of this world, that it brings at
once before us the truth, that here is not our
home. All religious feelings therefore are kindled up, and our habits of prayer and devotion
are quickened into exercise. And in this active,
busy age, when outward excitement has taken
the place of earnest, holy contemplation, how
necessary becomes any discipline, which can thus
withdraw us from the things of time and sense!
By its means we gather strength for the conflict
yet before us, in which " we wrestle not against
flesh and blood," but our enemies are those
mighty spirits who once bore a nobler nature
than our own — " powers which erst in Heaven
sat on thrones " — and who still, in their dark
apostacy, retain for the accomplishment of evil,
the same radiant intellects, with which they were
gifted for the service of God. We come forth
from our retirement, more subdued and chastened

thing according to his desire, and quietly to enjoy the
pleasures of life. There needs no more to expose him to
eternal misery."—Bishop WILSON, *Sacra Privata.* Wednesday.

in spirit—with a calm and abiding consciousness, that we must be the true followers of "the man of sorrows." Then, like His servants of old, to whom revelations came in the hours of holy abstinence, we are better prepared to listen to the voice of God — our own prayers go up more earnestly to His throne — and our affections are crucified to a world which is fast fleeting away. Therefore it was, that when the Church was reformed from the corruptions of Rome, fasting was still prescribed " to discipline the flesh, to free the spirit, and render it more earnest and fervent to prayer, and as a testimony and witness with us before God of our humble submission to His High Majesty, when we confess our sins unto Him, and are inwardly touched with sorrowfulness of heart, bewailing the same in the affliction of our bodies."[22] There is therefore, as much truth as poetry in the exhortation—

" Deem not such penance hard—thence from the soul
    The chords of flesh are loos'd, and earthly woes
Lose half their power to harm; while self-control
    Learns that blest freedom, which she only knows."[23]

[22] First part of the Homily on Fasting.
[23] *The Cathedral.*

Thus it is then that we may keep this Holy
Season — by withdrawing from the world — by
self-examination—by prayer and fasting—so that
when it has passed, we shall find that we have
gained new strength for our onward course.
And how strong the argument to do so, as one
year after another goes silently by, and we press
forward to the grave! Now indeed is our reward nearer than when first we believed. Now
is the bridegroom with some of us, almost at
hand. Soon we shall hear that warning cry,
which will startle even the slumbering from their
dreams, and then His train will sweep along, and
the glorious band of the Elect who are with Him,
go in to the marriage. But does each season, as
it thus bears us nearer to the tomb, carry us also
nearer to Heaven? Are we ready for that summons, with our account made up, and so living in
watchfulness that the coming of the Son of Man
can not surprise us? Are we numbered with
those "little ones" whose "angels do always
behold the face of our Heavenly Father," and
whom the Church, by the quiet influence of her
rites and services, is diligently training up for
immortality? When this decaying life is over,

and we are waiting in silence that stroke which
dismisses the spirit to its Judge, shall we be able
to feel, as we review our days, that we have
availed ourselves of all the opportunities our
Master afforded, of preparing for that solemn
crisis? Life with each one of us must be em-
ployed, in becoming meet for the recompense of
the just, and in gathering spoils for Eternity.
This is the only true use of existence here, and
thus only can it be something more tnan an
empty dream. It must be a life, spent in looking
forward to its close, and in preparing diligently
for that solemn change which is to pass upon all
men—

> " Life that shall send
> A challenge to its end,
> And when it comes, say ' Welcome, friend.' "

THE WEEK-DAY PRAYERS IN LENT..

Could ye not watch one hour!
Be ready! or the bridal train
And bridegroom, with His dower
May sweep along in vain.
  Miserere mei!
    Coxe's " *Christian Ballads.*"

III.

THE WEEK-DAY PRAYERS IN LENT.

"WHAT! could ye not watch with me one hour?" was on a certain occasion the appeal made to some of the disciples of our Master. And how solemnly must it have sounded in the ears of those to whom it was addressed! The Person from whom it came—the time—the place in which it was uttered — all united to invest it with emphasis. The Person was the Lord Jesus Christ. The time was when His career on earth was just closing, and the morrow was to behold Him stretched upon the Cross. The place was the garden of Gethsemane, the very name of which awakens in our minds, the remembrance of those fearful sorrows even unto death, of our suffering Lord.

We are told, that on that last night, after He

had instituted the sacred rite which was through
all ages, both to keep alive in the minds of His
people, the " perpetual memory of His precious
death and sacrifice until His coming again," and
also to be their " spiritual food and sustenance,"
He delivered His final instructions to the disciples, and then once more solemnly commended
them to the care of His Father who is in Heaven.
This was the concluding scene of His ministry,
and He therefore prepared Himself for the death
which was at hand. Taking Peter, and James, and
John, He went forth to the Garden, and " began
to be sorrowful and very heavy. Then saith He
unto them, My soul is exceeding sorrowful, even
unto death; tarry ye here, and watch with me.
And He went a little further, and fell on His
face, and prayed." And, oh ! how fearful was the
conflict of spirit which He then endured, when
the terrors of the death He was about to suffer,
were arrayed before His mind, and His human
nature was forced to shrink back from the view !
Listen to the earnest words of His petition, as
amid the darkness of the night, He prostrated
Himself upon the ground: " Father, all things
are possible unto Thee ; take away this cup from

me: nevertheless, not what I will, but what thou wilt." And then, "being in an agony, He prayed more earnestly; and His sweat was as it were great drops of blood falling down to the ground." It was when this prayer was ended — when he had poured out His soul to God, and been strengthened by an angel for His approaching trial, that returning to His disciples, He found them asleep, and awoke them with the mournful appeal — "What! could ye not watch with me one hour?"

And we think that our Lord might address this same touching inquiry to many among us, who in this day profess His name. There is too, in some respects, a degree of analogy between *our* situation, and that of the disciples who first listened to these words. We also are looking forward to that sacrifice on the Cross, the celebration of which will soon arrive. At this solemn season, we are—or ought to be—endeavoring by prayer, and weeping, and fasting, to prepare our hearts for uniting in its commemoration. And to aid us in this work, the Church has appointed peculiar services, well adapted to lead our thoughts away from the things of this world, to contemplate the mysteries of redemption. During each week in the season of Lent, in accordance with her regulations, the House of God is open, that his children may meet, and turn unto Him with that appropriate petition — " Create and make in us new and contrite hearts, that we, worthily lamenting our sins, and acknowledging our wretchedness, may obtain of Thee, the God of all mercy, perfect remission and forgiveness, through Jesus Christ our Lord."[1]

This then, is the most solemn period of our Ecclesiastical year, whether we look at the nature of the services in which we are invited to join, or that mysterious event to which we are constantly pointed forward. And yet, how seldom do even those who " profess and call themselves Christians," embrace as fully as they ought, these opportunities of communing with God in His holy temple ! How frequently, when the sanctuary each week opens its doors, and invites them to break off for a brief period from the bustle and engrossing cares of the world, do they permit the most trivial excuse to prevent them from answering to the call ! May not our Lord then

[1] Collect for Ash-Wednesday.

say to many among us, as He did to His disciples of old, in a tone of mingled sorrow and reproach — " What! could ye not watch with me one hour ! "

Let us then briefly look at some of the motives which should induce every Christian to avail himself of the week day services of the Church during this period.

THE SEASON ITSELF presents its earnest appeal. When God delivered the law upon Sinai, the people of Israel were commanded for three days before, to sanctify themselves, that they might be prepared to behold, even from a distance, the glory of Jehovah, as the mountain was wreathed with clouds, and " quaked greatly, because the Lord descended upon it in fire." When therefore we are called upon to approach that more wonderful mountain, on which, by the tears and blood of the Incarnate Son of God, was wrought out the sublime mystery of man's redemption, should we not be earnest to put away from us our earthliness of feeling, and to purify our hearts in anticipation of that solemn scene ? Yes, as the time draws near, when we are to be led to the Cross — to contemplate the Passion and bitter

agonies of our Lord — and to behold Him dying
for our salvation, it seems but proper, that we
should undergo some additional preparation of
heart. We should not rush at once from the
tumult of this noisy world, to the foot of Calvary.
When still far distant, we should veil our heads,
and put our shoes from off our feet, realizing
that we are on holy ground. As we slowly approach that spot, to which even angels would
look with intense emotion, a holy fear should fall
upon us, and in the depth of our souls we should
meditate upon the solemn scene which is to be
unfolded to our view.

Is it then asking too much, if during the brief
period of these forty days we are invited to assemble in the house of God more frequently, for a
short time to think of our dying Saviour, and to
bewail the sins which brought Him to the Cross?
Is there not an evident propriety in that regulation, commenced even in Primitive times, by which
Wednesday, (the day on which the Jews took
counsel to betray our Lord,) and Friday, (the
day of his death,) are peculiarly devoted to affectionate remembrance of Him, and humiliation

for ourselves?[2] Did He suffer in agony for our transgressions, and yet, shall we think so lightly of them, that we will not " rend our hearts," and pray God to blot out our guilt? Can we, while pursuing this course, realize as we should, the exceeding depth of our degradation? Can we truly estimate, from how fearful a woe we have been delivered, when we will not look to our Lord on the Cross, or remember how terrible were the sufferings which then crushed His human nature?

This indeed is a subject which appeals most plainly to our reason. Is there not every thing in the services, and the hallowed recollections of this period, to induce us to humble ourselves in the dust of abasement before God — to seek pardon for the past, and strength for the future? Should not every principle of gratitude to our Lord cause us to go gladly to the temple with

[2] St. Austin says—"This reason may be given, why the Church fasts chiefly on the fourth and sixth days of the week, because it appears upon considering the Gospel, that on the fourth day, which we commonly call *Feria Quarta*, the Jews took counsel to kill our Lord, and on the sixth day our Lord suffered. For which reason the sixth day is rightly appointed a fast."—BING. *Orig. Eccles.*, lib. xxi., chap. 3, sec. 2.

those that keep holyday? Should our public worship be confined to the Sunday; or should we not endeavor, by practice as well as by words, to show our concurrence in that sentence of the *Te Deum* which we so often repeat — " Day by day we magnify Thee!" When therefore all these appeals call forth no response from the hearts of our Lord's professed followers, may He not say to them — " ' What! could ye not watch with me one hour?' with *me*, who for your sake became ' a man of sorrows, and acquainted with grief' — with *me*, who was ' brought as a lamb to the slaughter,' that you might live? Must I disrobe myself of my Heavenly glory, and come to this earth of suffering and woe, and pass a weary pilgrimage of thirty years, and yet, my children not be able to watch one single hour, to prepare their hearts to think upon my sacrifice? Did I endure the crown of thorns — the scoffs of men — the malefactor's shame — and the agony of the Cross — and yet, are not those who. reap the benefit of my sufferings able to endure a single hour of communion with me — one single hour of watchfulness and prayer?"

Again — by attendance on the week-day

prayers, we are in some degree FOLLOWING THE
EXAMPLE SET US BY THE PRIMITIVE CHRISTIANS.
In the ancient Church, there were religious
assemblies for prayer and preaching every day
through the whole season of Lent. " I can not
affirm " — says Bingham — " that it was so in
every Parochial Church and country village, but
that it was so in the greater or Cathedral Churches,
is evident from undeniable proofs and matter of
fact."[8]

The Homilies of St. Chrysostom upon Genesis,
from which we have already so often quoted,
were sermons preached in this manner, day after
day, as is evident from many allusions they contain. Take, for example, a single passage in one
of them — " This is not the only thing that is
required, that we should meet here every day,
and hear sermons continually, and fast the whole
Lent. For if we gain nothing by these continual
meetings and exhortations and seasons of fasting
to the advantage of our souls, they will not only
do us no good, but be the occasion of a severer
condemnation. If after so much care and pains
bestowed upon us, we continue the same; if the

[8] *Orig. Eccles.*, lib. xxi, chap. 1, sec. 20.

angry man does not become meek, and the pas-
sionate mild and gentle; if the envious does not
reduce himself to a friendly temper; nor the cov-
etous man depart from his madness and fury in
the pursuit of riches, and give himself to alms-
deeds and feeding the poor; if the intemperate
man does not become chaste and sober, and the
vainglorious learn to despise false honor, and
seek for that which is true; if he that is negligent of charity to his neighbor, does not stir up
himself, and endeavor not only not to come behind the Publicans, (who love those that love
them,) but also to look friendly upon his enemies,
and exercise all acts of charity towards them;
if we do not conquer these affections, and all
others that spring up from our natural corruption; though we assemble here every day, and
enjoy continual preaching and teaching, and
have the assistance of fasting; what pardon can
we expect, what apology shall we make for ourselves?"[4]

Thus it was the custom of the Church, in her
primitive and holier days, by constantly recurring
periods of devotion, gradually to build up her

[4] St. Chrys. Hom. 11, in Gen., tom. ii., p. 107.

children in the faith, and in a ripeness of Christian character. Then, she so often called them to prayer, that the world had no opportunity of enlisting their affections, or leading them from the truth. They were forced to walk, " as seeing Him who is invisible." They devoted to intercourse with Heaven, and to communing with their own hearts before God, times which in this worldly age men could not bear to have snatched from secular employments. They were not contented with coming to their Lord's temple on the first day of each week alone, but they sanctified the hours of every day with devotion. Look, for instance, at what were called in the early Church, " the Canonical hours of Prayer,"[5]

[5] The subject of the daily services in the early Church deserves a brief notice, because in this day reference is often made to " the *seven* Canonical hours of public prayer in the Primitive Church," when in fact, no such seasons were known at that time. The appointed periods for daily prayer were probably *three* in number. One of the writers of the Oxford " Tracts for the Times," (who certainly would not be inclined to diminish these services of the early Church,) says " the Jewish observance of the third, sixth, and ninth hours for prayer, was continued by the inspired founders of the Christian Church. (*No.* 75, *on the Breviary.*) This also was Wheatley's view, (*On Common Prayer, p.* 84.) As late as the time of St. Chry-

by which without interfering with the business
of this world, she regularly called her members to
remember the solemn realities of the world which
is to come, and trained them up systematically

sostom, there is no mention in any writer of more than
these three periods. Thus in one place this Father represents an individual as complaining, " How is it possible for
me, who am a secular man, and confined to the courts of
law, to run to Church, *and pray at the three hours of the
day?*" To which St. Chrysostom answers, " that if he
could not come to Church, because he was so fettered to
the Court, yet he might pray even as he stood there."
(*Hom.* 4, *de Anna, tom.* ii., *p.* 995.) Tertullian also incidentally alludes to " tertia hora, et sexta, et nona," as the
usual ones of public prayer (*de Jejun., cap.* 10.)

The multiplication of these services began in the Eastern
Monasteries, among those who were cut off from secular
life, and whose time was entirely given up to devotion.
In this way, these appointed seasons were gradually expanded into what were called " the Seven Canonical Hours
of Prayer." Yet even in the fourth century, writers who
refer to the Six or Seven hours of prayer, speak of the
observance of the Monks only, and not of the whole body
of the Church. Such is the case frequently in St. Jerome's
works. From this beginning, these services were in latter
ages easily introduced into the principal Churches. We
believe therefore, that our own Church, with the arrangement for daily morning and evening prayers, is much
nearer the model of Primitive times, than those who
increased those services to Seven (See BINGHAM, lib. xiii.,
ch. 9, sec. 8.)

We refer here to the *public* services, for with regard to

for Heaven. " Unwavering, unflagging, not urged by fits and starts, not heralding forth their feelings, but resolutely, simply, perseveringly, day after day, Sunday and week-day, fast day and festival, week by week, season by season, year by year, in youth and in age, through a life, thirty years, forty years, fifty years, in prelude of the everlasting chant before the Throne — so they went on, ' continuing *instant* in prayer, after the pattern of Psalmists and Apostles, in the day with David, in the night with Paul and Silas, winter and summer, in heat and in cold, in peace and in danger, in a prison or in a cathedral, in the dark, in the day-break, at sun-rising, in the forenoon, at noon, in the afternoon, at eventide, and on going to rest, still they had Christ before them; His thought in their minds, His emblems in their eye, His name in their mouths, His service in their postures, magnifying Him and calling on all that lives to magnify Him, joining with Angels in Heaven and Saints in

the private devotions of the members of the Church we have reason to believe that the vivid picture given by Mr. Newman in the extract quoted above, is but a faithful view of their ordinary customs.

Paradise to bless and praise Him forever and ever.[6] It was this noble system which raised the early Church to that height of holiness, and enabled her to present her followers, as visibly crucified to the world.

But how different at this day is the spirit which prevails! The services of the sanctuary are looked upon too often, as being merely addressed to the intellect. We come to it, too much to listen to the preaching, and too little to commune with our God. We forget, that there it is man holds audience with the Deity. The consequence is, that while our Churches can be filled to listen merely to a human teacher, on prayer days there are but few scattered here and there, who feel the wish to abase themselves before God.[7] And the reason of this is evident. It is easy for individuals, to sit in their seats, and

[6] NEWMAN'S *Lectures on Justification*, p. 387.
[7] An old writer quaintly says — " To imagine that prayers at home will be as acceptable to God, as those made in the Church with our brethren, is as if one should have fancied, that the incense of the Temple (which was a compound of several precious gums,) made no other perfume than the spices would have done had they been burnt one by one."—(*Bishop* PATRICK *on Prayer*, p. 217.)

listen to the voice of the preacher. He is " unto
them as a very lovely song of one that hath a
pleasant voice, and can play well on an instrument." His sentences fall upon the ear, and it
is a pleasant excitement, to have the intellect
aroused, and the imagination addressed, but it is
not easy to pray. It requires effort to command
the wandering thoughts — to shut out an intru-
sive world — to keep the mind intently fixed on
God — and to kneel before him with a calm, collected, and awakened soul. To have the continual spirit of prayer, is not shown by now and
then sending up glowing petitions to Heaven,
when the mind is for a time excited. It is something far different from these paroxysms of devotion. It is to come daily before God, in a solemn,
serious frame, realizing that He " readeth our
thoughts, and trieth our hearts," and that " His
saints and angels,"[8] even " a great cloud of wit-

[8] The Apostle Paul, when declaring (1 Cor. xi. 10,)
that a woman should cover her head in time of Prayer,
" because of the Angels," certainly seems to intimate, that
at such times these heavenly visitants are about us. So
at least this passage was looked upon by the ancient
Christians, and it gave them great encouragement to attend
upon the public Prayers. The same idea is curiously

nesses compass us about." This therefore is the very discipline we need, and by which the Church endeavors to have wrought into our souls, the spirit of holiness.

There is indeed a subduing influence in Prayer, which a careless world seems never to know. The very sound of " the Church-going bell," speaks to the heart, and recalls us from our earthly feelings. As its solemn tones fall upon the ear, they seem like a voice from eternity, telling us of realities, while we wander in a world of shadows. Beautiful therefore was that superstition of the Middle Ages, which ascribed to them the power of driving far off the Evil Spirits which gather about the path of man, to tempt him to sin. As the deep sound of the evening bell was heard upon the breeze, and the sweet tones of the Vesper Hymn floated indistinctly to

stated by Origen in his comments on those words of the Psalmist—" the Angel of the Lord encampeth round about them that fear Him." " It is probable "—says he—" that when many are assembled together sincerely to the glory of Christ, the angel of every one of them there pitcheth his tent, together with him who is committed to his charge and custody; so as to make a *double Church*, where the saints are gathered together; one Church of men, and another Church of angels."

the traveler's ear, his heart was strengthened within him, and he felt, that here at least, where that holy sound came, spiritual enemies had no power. Yet not entirely was this a superstition. The wild legends which embody it teach also a deep moral to the thoughtful mind, and one which a Poet of our own hath set forth, arrayed in all that beauty with which genius can invest the truth.

> I have read in the marvelous heart of man,
> That strange and mystic scroll,
> That an army of phantoms, vast and wan,
> Beleaguer the human soul.
>
> Encamped beside Life's rushing stream,
> In Fancy's misty light,
> Gigantic shapes and shadows gleam
> Portentous through the night.
>
> But when the solemn and deep Church bell,
> Entreats the soul to pray,
> The midnight phantoms feel the spell,
> The shadows sweep away.
>
> Down the broad Vale of Tears afar,
> The spectral camp is fled;
> Faith shineth as a morning star,
> Our ghastly fears are dead.[9]

How wise then is that provision of the Church,

[9] LONGFELLOW'S *Beleaguered City.*

by which she calls us to these oft-recurring prayers! She wishes thus, to render us "meet to be partakers of the inheritance of the saints in light." It is for this reason too, that she so frequently in her Calendar commemorates the holy dead, who have already entered into their rest. Contracted indeed is the view of this subject which so many take, when they inquire, Why should we pay this reverence to "men of like passions with ourselves?" And yet do not these compose that "noble army," which gathers around the Christian pilgrim as he travels onward, and whom he may well remember as his bright examples? Is it not right therefore, as the year rolls round, that one by one they should meet him in the services of the Church, that he may thus be enabled to think of their self-denying labors, their holy lives, and their patient sufferings? The Church in this is but following the example of St. Paul, when in the eleventh chapter of his epistle to the Hebrews, he summons up, as with a trumpet's voice, name after name of those departed worthies who had long gone to their reward. And since his day, how gloriously has the list been extended, as the

Gospel dispensation presents its holy array of apostles, and saints, and just men made perfect, until the long and bright procession passes before us, stirring our hearts up to a holy emulation.

But their example is not all. It is thus that we are reminded also of the dignity of our warfare. The Christian is too apt, in times of depression, to feel himself a solitary, and it may be, a derided traveler. He looks upon himself as standing isolated in a hostile world. These services then are like a chain, which connects him with the holy dead who have gone before. He finds, that he has inherited his privileges from martyrs and confessors—from kings of the earth, its princes, and its judges, who in their generation " fought the good fight," and then were gathered into the Paradise of God. His feelings of loneliness pass away. He realizes, that he is one of a great company, which embraces in its ranks all that is pure and dignified in the universe, and his heart rejoices in " the communion of saints."[10]

---

[10] " The thought of the dead makes us gentle and childlike, and leads us to forget ourselves, as well it may. For know that according to St. Paul's teaching the spirits of just men made perfect are not far from us. We are come

" Thus, though oft depressed and lonely,
　　All his fears are laid aside,
　　If he but remembers only
　　Such as these have lived and died."

And here, we can not forbear quoting from one
of the most admirable works of this generation—
the only one we know giving the portraiture of
a Christian family—a passage showing the manner in which these Festivals can be profitably
observed. " For example, I take up the character of St. Peter for my especial meditation, which
most probably, but for this notice of it by the
Church, I never should have done; at least, I
should have rested content with the vague, tran-
sitory, and unpractical notions suggested in the
course of turning over, amid a multitude of others

to them, and they are come to us. They can touch us,
and we can touch them; they are gliding by every hour.
The spirit has but ceased to act upon and through the
body, and so we do not see them in their places. They
keep threading in and out among us, going up and down,
and moving round about us; especially, so we believe from
St. John, in holy Churches where their bodies rest in hope.
(Rev. vi.) They are the first ranks of the Church, who
have gone before us in the Lord, so far as to be out ot
sight. They are beyond our view. They may see us; we
can not see them."—FABER's Tracts on the *Offices of the
Church.*

in Scripture, the passages which relate to him. But now I turn it in every possible light, refer to the minutest incident, analyzing and composing, till I frame to myself an adequate conception of his character. I then examine myself by it, and review his ardent and courageous spirit till I imbibe some portion of it myself, and discuss his temporary fall till I arrive at a wholesome fear of my own weakness; and on coming to his restoration, so completely do I feel identified with him, I rejoice and glorify his blessed Master, and my own, as if I had been restored together with him. And, last of all, I look intently upon that death, which according to his Master's prediction he underwent, and prepare myself also to take up the Cross of my Lord, and fear Him, and not man. All these thoughts may have passed through my mind often before; but it was in a floating, undirected, unpractical mass, and not arranged as now, in clusters, under suitable heads, tending to one definite end, and by the point given to them, leaving their impression distinct and deep, both on memory and feelings. Besides, by thus steadily following one train, I am led at last, to ideas on the subject, and com binations of ideas which had never before presented themselves; and I experience with the increase of my spiritual knowledge an accession also of mental wealth. At a due interval arrives another festival, the centre of attraction to another class of thoughts, which had else been too loose and vague to produce any impression; these too I fix in permanence. In this manner I am carried round the year; my views grow clearer, my resolutions more firm; such days are to me indeed holy days; in them I find a secure repose for my thoughts from the vulgar turmoil of the world around, to which I return at least refreshed, and I hope I may add, improved."[11]

The Church, it is true, in these services offers us no excitement. She never teaches that glowing devotion, (or what is miscalled devotion,) which on Sunday lifts its possessor up to the very gates of Heaven, yet during the week is never visible in his conduct. Her aim is to instruct us in a sober, constant, and Scriptural piety. She employs no spiritual whirlwind now and then to sweep over her, which when it has subsided, leaves her children during the remainder of the

[11] *Rectory of Valehead*, p. 54.

year, to sink back again to a death-like coldness,
but she goes on the even tenor of her way,
steadily building them up in a knowledge of the
faith. Neither indeed does she present us with
any novelties, for the prayers and praises in which
we unite, have been heard in her services a long
time, some of them for more than fourteen centuries.[12] They are a precious legacy, bequeathed
to us by ages which have gone. They are "the
form of sound words" which our fathers used,
and with which the dead in Christ were accustomed to worship a thousand years ago. Thus
it is, that her voice is lifted up through all the
changing year, and we are but prolonging that
anthem of praise, which has always been heard
in her courts. The very words we utter, carry
us back to days when the faith of the Church
was purified by suffering. They connect us in

[12] For instance, the prayer of St. Chrysostom, at the
close of the service. Also, the Doxologies, the Trisagion
or cherubical hymn, Holy, Holy, Holy, &c., and the Mag-
nificat. The Te Deum has been generally ascribed to St.
Ambrose, although some learned men have disputed this.
For a particular account of the most noted hymns in use
in the service of the ancient Church, see BINGHAM's *Orig
Eccles.*, lib., xiv., chap. 2.

thought and Spirit with those of whom the world was not worthy, who have long since passed away to their reward.   ·

Again — another reason why every Christian should avail himself of these services is, THAT HE MAY DRAW DOWN A BLESSING UPON HIS CHURCH. We meet at such times, to humble ourselves not merely as individuals, but also as a Church. In this respect, we have surely much to bewail for the time that is gone. Like Israel of old, we too may " remember our ways, and be ashamed." Compared with the opportunities placed in our hand, how little have we done as a Church, to advance the cause of pure and undefiled religion! With thousands in our own land straying into heresy and schism, and millions on the wastes of heathenism " perishing for lack of knowledge," how little through us has the glad news of our Redeemer's sacrifice been published through the earth, or the sweet incense of His name been borne to the hearts of the dying! Have we not sins then as a Church to confess? And when can we more appropriately remember these our deficiencies, than when we are preparing to cele- brate that sacrifice, around which are gathered

our own hopes of eternal life, and which was intended to bring salvation to all who will avail
themselves of its benefits!

If we wish then, that the ultimate triumph of
the Gospel should not be held back through any
fault of ours, is it not well that we should call
upon God for strength to enable us to fulfill our
recorded vows, and to realize the interest which
we have in the spiritual welfare of our race?
There is indeed no better instrument than prayer,
to aid the progress of our Master's cause. When
we look over the world, and see how iniquity
abounds, and the love of many waxes cold, we
feel at times tempted to despond and to let the
conflict go on. But Scripture teaches us a different lesson with regard to the power of prayer.
St. Paul writes to the Thessalonians—"Brethren!
pray for us, that the word of God may have free
course and be glorified." And in accordance with
this, the Church directs us to offer up petitions
" for all sorts and conditions of men." She
even instructs us to pray for spiritual blessings
upon ourselves, only that they may be imparted
to others also. The language of her Evening
Anthem is—" God be merciful unto us, and bless

us, and show us the light of His countenance
and be merciful unto us." And why? "That
Thy way may be known upon earth, Thy saving
health among all nations." We find then, that
we also as a Church have, in this respect a duty
to perform with regard to the advancement of
our faith.

And here we would remark more particularly
on the duty of presenting our petitions to God,
for those who attend with us in the same sanctuary. When we remember how often the Gospel
is proclaimed in our Churches, and that it is
God's own appointed means for publishing the
truth, we can not but ask, Why is it that so few
receive it? Why do the majority of those who
listen, still refuse to be reconciled to our Lord,
or be numbered with his followers?. Must there
not be guilt resting on those who " profess and
call themselves Christians," that they do not
petition Him to pour out upon our Churches
"the healthful spirit of His grace?" If the voice
of prayer were not restrained, we should witness
no spiritual desolation, but " God. even our God,
would give us His blessing." Let those then who
believe that they are " children of the light and

of the day," think how much they owe to the
love of Him who hath called them to His service.
Who made them to differ from the thousands
around, who are still seeking to draw comfort
from this vain world, and wasting their strength
in pursuit of its fleeting shadows? Who opened
their eyes to see the solemn realities of eternity,
and put a new song in their mouth, filling them
with the rich comforts of His grace? Let us
think too of the state of those, who are still without the ark of safety — How blindly they are
rushing on to an inheritance of woe—how they
are standing in jeopardy every hour, reckless of
the storm which is gathering against them—and
our sympathies will be awakened in their behalf.
Then, we shall need no other inducement to
" watch for one hour" with the people of God,
where prayer is offered up, that we also may
present that appropriate petition—" Return, we
beseech Thee, O God of hosts: look down from
Heaven, and behold, and visit this vine, and the
vineyard which Thy right hand hath planted,
and the branch that Thou madest strong for
Thyself."

There is one other motive which pleads with

us, to avail ourselves of the solemnities of this
Season.   It is the truth, THAT WE MAY NOT LIVE
TO SEE AGAIN THE RETURN OF THIS PERIOD OF OUR
ECCLESIASTICAL YEAR.   This may be our last Lent
on earth, to herald in either an eternal Festival
in Heaven, or to be but the prelude to that
" lamentation and mourning and woe," in which
the desolate spirit can look forward to no joyful
Easter.   But the reflection, that life is passing
rapidly away, and that its continuance is uncertain, although often brought before us, is still one
which to most, is any thing but familiar.   The
remembrance of it, as a fact, exerts but little
practical influence over our thoughts and our
conduct.   We acknowledge it as a general truth,
and yet silently make an exception in our own
favor.   Let us endeavor then, to bring it home
to our own hearts and consciences, as a reality
in which we have a deep and fearful interest.
And how solemn — how awakening should be
the effect of the thought, that we may be passing
through this period of improvement for the last
time—that when the next year the people of the
Lord are thus summoned to come up, and make
ready for the celebration of His Passion, we may

not hear the call! Then, our probation may
have ended—our account be sealed up against
the Great Day of moral retribution — and our
graves in the quiet Churchyard, be growing
green amidst the graves of our kindred. And
yet, this is possible with all who witness the services of this season, and certain with regard to
some. It would be strange indeed, if even
among those who may read these pages, some
should not be borne to their last resting-place
before twelve months have rolled round. Think
of those who at this time last year sat in the
same seats with us in the temple of God, but
who have now departed forever. Can not memory recall the images of some who have since
then passed from our own little circle to the
silence of the tomb, and whose familiar forms and
faces we shall see no more, until that mighty ·
word goes forth, which heard on sea and land
shall call up the dust of the sepulchre to new
life, and mould it again into its ancient shapes?
Yes, the Destroyer has been among us, since last
with joy we sang together our Easter anthem.
In many a household there have been bitter
lamentations for the dead; and a vacant seat by

the hearth, and an added tombstone in the
Churchyard are the sole earthly memorials of
some, who in the weeks of the last year's Lent
were often found in the house of God. The loved
ones are not all here. Smiles of affection which
once were ready to greet us, and tones which fell
like music on our ears, have faded away from the
earth. The dust has claimed its own, and our
hearts even now turn in sorrow to the place of
graves, where the dead so silently await our
coming.

And of whom shall this history next be written? Do we all shrink from the question, and
feel we can not bear to realize that this may be
the case with us? Do we close our ears, as the
solemn tones of life's curfew bell are heard,
warning us of the gathering night? Oh, let us
remember, that we have no exemption from this
common lot, and that the Master may come in
an hour when we look not for Him. With the
flush of health upon the cheek, and the vigor of
manhood in the limbs, we may be unconsciously
treading the edge of the crumbling precipice,
about to be launched into Eternity.

———————— Time is fleeting,
And our hearts, though stout and brave,
Still like muffled drums are beating
Funeral marches to the grave.[18]

Let the determination then be strengthened within us, that while life lasts, we will neglect no opportunity of making ready for our solemn change — that if it should be decreed in the councils of Heaven, that we shall never again on earth witness this interesting season in the Church, this at least shall not be neglected, but we will repair to the House of God, there to pour out our souls in the prayer of penitence and faith.

Are not these then motives enough to induce us to take our part in these week-day services? Methinks our Lord is thus age after age, even from the garden of Gethsemane, lifting up to His faithful followers the voice alike of entreaty and of agony, saying unto them — "What! could ye not watch with me one hour!" And is it not our business here, to train ourselves for the ceaseless worship of Heaven? Are we then gaining this spirit of prayer which will render us "meet to be partakers of the inheritance of the saints

[18] LONGFELLOW'S *Psalm of Life.*

in light?"   Let us examine our own hearts, and
scrutinize our affections, lest we may be deceived,
and the spirituality and holiness of the Christian
be still wanting in our breasts.   Neither is it all
that is necessary, merely to be bodily present in
the House of God, for we may at the same time
"be absent in spirit," and thus in our best services be accumulating guilt.   He whom we mock
with the offering of the lips while the heart is
far from Him, will say to us, as He did to His
ancient people—" The calling of assemblies I can
not away with: it is iniquity, even the solemn
meeting."   The world therefore must be shut
out—the spirit of devotion must be with us—or
we are not truly watching with our Lord.

   And should there chance to rest upon these
pages, the eye of any one who does not profess
to be a disciple of our once suffering but now
•glorified Master, and who therefore may feel dis-
posed to pass by this appeal as being in his case
inapplicable, we would address to him also a
single inquiry.   Have you no need of prayer —
no necessity for that atonement on the Cross, to
which these services point us forward?   If such
are your feelings, the disclosures of a coming day

will show, that you have been the victim of a
fatal delusion. We look beyond the few remaining days of this fleeting life — we stand with our
fellow men before the bar of God — we behold
" the Lamb slain from the foundation of the
world " — but what is the condition of those,
who have no interest in his Redemption ? For
them there is no song of triumph — no victor's
crown. They are arrayed before their Judge in
speechless despair. The neglected opportunities
of earth are rising in their memories, and they
feel that they would give the universe, were it
possible, for " one hour " of that probation which
once they trifled away. The future offers to them
no gleam of hope, but shrinking from " the Great
White Throne, and the face of Him that sitteth
thereon," they commence the desolate travel of
Eternity — lost — undone forever.

We would entreat you then, O restless and
disappointed child of immortality ! to avail yourself of this solemn season, when all things invite
you to thoughtfulness and prayer. Turn away
from this decaying, perishing world, whose enchantments only mock your sight, and whose
promised blessings fade and disappear while you

seek to grasp them, and gain in their place, "the
peace which passeth understanding"—the calm
and solid happiness which our faith only can be·
stow. It is to be found—not in feverish and vain
desires—not in the aspirings of wild ambition—
not amid the rush and hurry of this busy life—
but in the whispers of an approving conscience,
and in silent communion with your God. Come
then, and in a spirit of earnest supplication, pray
Him to blot out the dark record of the past, and
to strengthen you for his service during the years
which may yet remain to you on earth. Come,
before life is departing, and the terror-stricken
soul seeks in vain for a single hour in which to
make its peace with Him. Come, before the
darkness of the grave gathers around, and the
despairing cry is heard — "Woe unto us! for the
day goeth away, for the shadows of the evening
are stretched out."

HOLY WEEK.

Thus everywhere we find our suffering God,
  And where He trod
May set our steps; the Cross on Calvary
  Uplifted high
Beams on the martyr host, a beacon light
  In open fight.

                                        KEBLE.

IV.

HOLY WEEK.

JERUSALEM was crowded with thronging thousands, for the Great Festival of the year was at hand. From every part of Judea they had come up to the Holy City, that face to face the distant tribes might greet each other and brighten that chain of brotherhood which linked them together as one nation. The Passover drew nigh and this was the time of preparation. Yet—although they knew it not —never was there a Passover like unto that. It even exceeded in solemnity the first celebration of that rite, when they ate the Lamb in Egypt as they were about to go forth from servitude, with the Angel of Death hovering over their houses, while the wail of the stricken Egyptians came mournfully to their ears,

because "there was not a house where there
was not one dead." From that time they had
kept the feast—in the wanderings of the desert
and in the enjoyments of their own land—when
captives by the rivers of Babylon and amid the
glories of their own Holy City. For centuries
the Paschal Lamb had died, pre-figuring that
Lamb of God who was to take away the sins
of the world. But now, "the fulness of time"
had come. The reality of all these symbols—
the accomplishment of all these types—the ful·
filment of all ancient prophecies, was at hand.
The Great Antitype walked among His people,
though they looked on Him only as a peasant
of Galilee. The true Paschal Lamb was ready
to be offered, and the hour drew nigh when the
Sacrifice should be consummated.

Eighteen centuries have gone by since that
Festival of the Jews. The Holy City has
become the prey of the fierce idolator, the
tribes of Israel have been scattered, and no
more is the Passover celebrated as of old. Yet
it has only changed its form, because with us it
is no longer the anticipation of some coming
sacrifice, but the commemoration of one that is

passed. The Church, therefore, still continues it from age to age, and as Holy Week comes round, she prepares for the solemn service of Good Friday, that thus she may celebrate the crucifixion of her Lord.

But do we truly keep the preparation for this Christian Passover? The Jew devoted days beforehand to making ready for its coming. All the rites of his ceremonial law were most scrupulously observed, for he who failed in the least point was rendered unclean and prevented from participating in the feast. But are we as earnest to be spiritually pure as were the Jews that they should be ceremonially clean? Do we—in the Apostle's words —" Keep the feast, not with old leaven, neither with the leaven of malice and wickedness, but with the unleavened bread of sincerity and truth "? Do we put off our worldliness, so that when we approach the Cross, it is with hearts chastened with godly fear; or, do we rush with all our earthly hopes and wishes, from the tumult of this passing life to the very presence of our Lord? Is it not true, that as years have rolled on and time has borne us

7

farther from the event which took place on that Passover, we have ceased to regard it with that awe which once inspired our Lord's followers? Holy Week comes and we do not realize that it is the very crowning season of the Christian year, that around it should be gathered and clustered all our hopes. And now that we have once more reached it, let us look to the former days and see how in earlier and purer times this Holy Season was kept, that thus from the contrast we may learn our own deficiencies.

In Primitive times, the very titles they gave to this season showed their reverence. It was called the PASSION WEEK, because then we celebrate the blessed Passion of our Lord, by which redemption was wrought out for the world. It was called the HOLY WEEK, because then was the very crisis of the world's spiritual history—the very agony of that contest for its rule which was fought between the powers of light and darkness,—and all of holiness this earth shall ever have is owing to the solemn sacrifice which at that time was offered up. · "It was called the GREAT WEEK," says

St. Chrysostom, "not because it consists of longer days, or more in number than other weeks, but because at this time great things were wrought out for us by our Lord. For in this week the ancient tyranny of the Devil was dissolved, Death was extinct, the strong man was bound, his goods were spoiled, sin was abolished, the curse was destroyed, Paradise was opened, Heaven became accessible, men and angels were joined together, the middle wall of partition was broken down, the barriers were taken out of the way, the God of peace made peace between things in Heaven and things on earth; therefore it is called the Great Week." [1]

The first feature then which we notice in the observance of this Week in primitive times was —THE ENTIRE SUSPENSION OF ALL WORLDLY OCCUPATIONS. This was to them the Great Sab-bath of the Year—that period around which they had gathered all their hopes—and there-fore, like the first day of the week, they care-fully set it apart for religious observances. The public games of the circus and amphitheatre,

[1] *Hom. in Psal.* 145.

which formed the great amusements of the people and to which, at other times, they were accustomed daily to resort, was then denied them, as being inconsistent with that season when our Lord was going through His bitter agony. And for the same reasons all legal proceedings were prohibited, except in the case of the manumission of slaves, which being an act of charity was allowed at all seasons.[2] There was indeed at this time a solemn pause in all the ordinary business of life, and every heart was occupied with that approaching day when in sorrow they celebrated the Passion of their Lord. That was their preparation for this crowning season of the Christian year.

And now, look at our case. The centuries which have rolled by have not made the Sacrifice of our Lord less precious—nay, if any comparison might be drawn with regard to so solemn a theme—they have increased its power, for now its efficacy is each year applied to greater numbers, as the Church is gathering new millions into her fold. But yet we seem to lose our regard for the solemn season when all this

[2] *Bingham, iv.,* 125.

was wrought out. We can keep an earthly Festival—the day of a nation's freedom—with every mark of honor; but that day when we were freed from the dominion of sin and Satan —when the way was opened for us to become the children of the light—is little regarded. We cannot rescue it from the world. We cannot withdraw this Holy Week from our secular pursuits. We cannot make it different from the ordinary weeks of life, but one "goeth to his farm and another to his merchandise," and all would hold themselves excused from surrendering up so much time to their Lord.

But look, on the other hand, how beautiful and at the same time how reasonable is the theory of the Church. She wishes to impress upon you the wonderful acts of our Lord's grace—to familiarize your minds with all the solemn scenes through which He passed—that thus your deepest interest may be excited, as you follow Him on to the Cross at Calvary. When therefore the closing scenes are at hand and you stand on the threshold of the very week thus made memorable through all time, she calls you to a deeper devotion—to a more perfect withdrawal from the world.

And can you, in any other way, walk with your Lord? Can you not imagine that, as the preparation for this Passover drew nigh, He experienced a deeper intensity of feeling when He looked forward to His approaching sacrifice? When He turned His face toward Jerusalem and went up to the Festival, it was not like St. Paul, when he said " he knew not the things that should befall him there." Our Lord, on the contrary, realized perfectly that the Holy City was to be to Him the theatre of His sufferings and death. And the depth of His emotions—the added sorrow which weighed down His spirit—we can behold in the final scenes of His pilgrimage. As we read the narrative of His life, we evidently see that the clouds gathered more darkly about Him as His sun was setting. What unequalled tenderness was breathed forth in His last prayer with His disciples ! What a solemnity marked His participation in the Passover, when He changed the object of that rite and made it to His people henceforth significant of His death ! What un-

speakable anguish racked Him in the scenes of
the Garden ! And this constituted His prepara·
tion for the shame of the Judgment Hall and
the agony of the Cross.

And now we are entering on the time marked
by these very scenes. Each day of Holy Week
should bring to our minds the remembrance
of something connected with these sufferings.
They pass before us like a Mighty Drama, but
one in which every human being has a deep
personal interest. We see the catastrophe from
the beginning—for prophets in the elder days
had marked it out—and we feel its influence at
every step, as we advance along the solemn ave·
nue which closes at Calvary. The sorrows of
the Son of God seem so mighty as almost to ex·
clude all earthly feeling. His end is fixed on
high, and He passes in sublime composure to
fulfil His destiny. His agony is awful—His
death a sacrifice for the good of the universe.
Every step, therefore, is marked by a lofty con-
secration. Every thing is invested with a sanc·
tity which makes even bodily pain sublime.[3]
And shall we look on these things, and then

[3] *Retros. Review.*

turn away at once to our worldly cares? Alas, how much have we wandered from the devotion of early days, when this solemn season meets with so little notice, and Holy Week to us is like the weeks of this ordinary life!

Again—another way in which this week was kept by the Primitive Church was—BY MULTI-PLIED RELIGIOUS SERVICES. They met every day, not only for prayer, but for preaching and re-ceiving the Holy Communion.[4] Thus, St. Chry-sostom says, "For seven days together we hold religious assemblies, and prepare a spiritual ta-ble for you, making you partakers of the Divine Oracles, and every day anointing you with the Spiritual unction of instruction, arming you against the Devil. Seven days together ye have preaching, that ye may learn perfectly to wres-tle with your enemy."[5] And he calls the whole solemnity a Spiritual Marriage, which, after the manner of other marriage solemnities, lasted seven days.

And so far was this carried, that an early Council decreed—" On those six most Holy Days

[4] *Bingham, ix.,* 123.
[5] *Chrys. de Resur. Christi.*

let no one presume to do any servile labor, but
let all with one consent attend the Service of
the Paschal Festival, and persevere in offering
up their Daily Sacrifices, praising Him who
created and redeemed us, both Evening and
Morning and at Noon-Day." [6]

In this respect, too, we perceive that the
Church endeavors to follow Primitive practice,
and therefore, through every day of this week,
she invites us to come to her courts and join in
her solemn services, providing an Epistle and
Gospel for each Morning Service. Would that
her members were equally anxious to imbibe the
spirit of ancient times! " The early Christians
really worshipped. They went out of their own
minds into the Infinite Temple which was around
them. They saw Christ in the Gospels, in the
Creed, in the Sacraments, and other rites; in
the visible structure and ornaments of His house,
in the Altar, and in the Cross; and not content
with giving the service of their eyes, they gave
Him their voices, their bodies, and their time—
gave up their rest by night, and their leisure by
day, all that could evidence the offering of their

* *Bingham, ix.,* 124.

7*

hearts to Him. Theirs was not a service once a week, or some one day now and then painfully given, but every day and every portion of the day was begun and sanctified with devotion." [7]

We perceive, then, how widely different this was from the custom of our day, when men come fitfully to the house of God, but as soon as they have left it, gather up their energies once more for their worldly pursuits and rush on in the same path as before. The hour of prayer seems scarcely to produce a break in the current of their worldly feelings. These services, therefore, fail in their object, nor will a careless occasional attendance in any way produce the influence they are intended to effect. Their object is, to promote the growth of a feeling of devotion, to create, as it were, a new element in our fallen and apostate nature, gradually detaching it from this earth and forming new associations which lead it forward to Heaven.

And how can we apply this truth better than in urging the observance of this Holy

[7] *Newman.*

Week? If in the weeks that have gone by you have been regular in your attendance on the services of the Church, with the right spirit coming up to its Holy Courts, then you have prepared yourself for the more frequent devo-. tions to which you are now invited. Then, if true to yourself, you have made ready to meet your Master, and as, day by day, the lesson of His trial and suffering is read before you, it will not fall on ears that are deaf or hearts which this world hath trampled into hardness. Your sympathies will flow forth, will gather around the Cross. To you, it will be a living, life-giving sign, and when this Holy Season is gone, you will look at the hours spent in the Temple, and as you go on your way with added strength, realize that for you it was good to have been there.

One more way, we would mention, in which the members of the Early Church marked this season was, BY MORE ABUNDANT GOOD WORKS. They were earnest, at this time, to show their liberality to the poor, nothing being thought more suitable to the occasion, than for men to make the hearts of the poor rejoice, at the time when they remembered the Common Fountain of their mercies. "In this week," says St. Chrysostom, "many increase their labors; some adding to their fastings, others to their watch· ings; others give more liberal alms, testifying the greatness of the Divine Goodness by their care of good works and more intense piety of holy living."[8]

This (as we mentioned before) was the season chosen too, to manumit their slaves, that they might be not only free men in Christ Jesus, but free men also from their worldly servitude.[9]

The Emperors also at this time were accus· tomed to grant a general release to all prison· ers, except such as it would be a scandal to pardon, because their actions would be a re· proach to the purity of this Holy Season. "For who," says the Emperor Valentinian, in his Decree, when making this exception, "would grant an Indulgence to one guilty of sacrilege, at a Holy Season? Who would pardon an impure person at a time which calls for perfect chastity? Let, too, the poisoner

[8] *Chrys. Hom. in Psal.* 145.
[9] *Bingham, ix.,* 121.

and the Sorcerer still suffer, and let the murderer expect the same that he has done to others." But except these criminals, all others had the benefit of the public pardon at this solemn season. And St. Chrysostom, in one of his Lent Sermons, thus gives the reason of this custom. "The Imperial Letters are sent abroad at this time, commanding all prisoners to be set at liberty from their chains. For as our Lord, when He descended into Hell, set free those that were detained by Death, so the servants, according to their power, imitating the kindness of their Lord, loose men from their corporeal bonds, when they have no power to relax the spiritual."

Those, indeed, were days when a Christian's faith was measured by his good works, not by his own estimate of his passing feelings. Christianity was marked by heroic virtues and lofty impulses, which made her charity go forth in manifold channels of mercy. Her children then were proved by being the bearers of spiritual and temporal aid to the poor and ignorant. Holy employments and works of benevolence seemed something in harmony with the faith.

Those days are gone, the times are dark, and a curtain of gloom hangs over the future. Shall those ages of faith ever return? If they do it will be because the Church turns from the worldliness of these present days to the loftier conduct of early times. Let us begin, then, at this season, to look to a higher standard of Christian action. Acts of self-denial can always be done. The poor we have always with us, claiming relief. The Church of God, crippled in every movement, asks our aid. Let us put forth our hands then to this holy labor, and verily I say unto you, we shall not have finished the work set before us before the Son of Man come.

Thus it was that the Early Church kept this Holy Week. "As the Jews," says St. Chrysostom, in the Homily from which we have already quoted, "went forth to meet Christ when He had raised Lazarus from the dead, so now, not one city, but all the world go forth to meet Him, not with palm branches in their hands, but with Alms-deeds, Humanity, Virtue, Fasting, Tears, Prayers, Watchings, and all kinds of piety, which they offer to Christ, their Lord." How

beautiful, then, this picture which has come
down to us through so many centuries—the inhabitants of all Christendom, with one heart
and one voice, going forth to meet their Lord,
as He comes to them in the scenes of His Passion, His garments wet with blood like him that
treadeth the wine-press! How forcibly does it
reveal to us alike the unity of the Church, and
the devotion of its members!

And do we not as Christians feel the necessity of these solemn services to aid us in shutting
out the world more and more from our affections, since soon there must come a time when
we are to leave this shifting scene forever?
Should we not prize every opportunity of preparing for this last and solemn change? And
should we not give the benefit of our example
to those around who as yet take but little interest in those themes which soon to them will be
everything? If they find us too much immersed
in the world, too busy with life's earthly cares,
to withdraw from them for a few hours during
this Holy Week, what is the lesson conveyed
to them? Give them not occasion, O servant of
the Lord, because you are recreant to your duty,

to drown the voice of conscience or shun the path in which they should walk. Permit them not, at the last day, to rise up and point to you, as one whose prevailing worldliness caused them to disregard the means of grace and fail in obtaining an inheritance with the saints; but rather show, by your regularity in God's House, that you prize the ordinances of this Holy Week, and that to you it shall be, indeed, the preparation for the Christian Passover.

GOOD FRIDAY.

Low bow'd Thy head convulsed, and droop'd in death,
    Thy voice sent forth a sad and wailing cry;
Slow struggled from Thy breast the parting breath,
    And every limb was wrung with agony.
        That head whose veil-less blaze
        Filled angels with amaze,
When at that voice sprang forth the rolling suns on high.

Milman's "Hymn to the Saviour."

V.

GOOD FRIDAY.

"AND they crucified Him." Simple yet solemn words! telling in this little expression of the most fearful event which has ever taken place upon this globe, since at the hour of its first creation "the morning stars sang together, and all the sons of God shouted for joy," as they joined in that glorious jubilee. And how vividly does this short sentence bring before us that terrible scene — fit conclusion to the long years of self-denial and sorrow—when the Son of God bowed Himself upon the Cross, and with an agony of which no man can conceive, passed the gates of Death! The imagination calls up the mighty crowd which had gathered to that spectacle — the jibe and scorn of the Jewish priests, as they inflamed the bigoted and urged on the shrinking — the whirl and roar of scoffing thousands, as that living flood poured out from the Holy City, and rolled around the sacred Mount. And far above them, "lifted up to be seen of all men," on the only throne which His rebellious subjects gave, was the promised Messiah, hearing even in death their mad ingratitude and cruel tauntings. Yet on that patient sufferer's brow, where the inspiration of the Divinity and the agonies of Humanity struggled together, we may believe, there beamed an expression of the loftiest triumph. He felt, that even in dissolution He was winning the noblest victory, and gaining immortality for the countless tribes of His fellow men.

As the hours passed on, popular passion was stirred up to its wildest excess. The rude uproar and furious execration of myriads filled the air, and mingled with the low, deep tones of our expiring Master, while He prayed for His enemies, or commended His soul to God. At length, there rang without the walls of Jerusalem that last, loud cry, which proclaimed to a wondering universe, that all was finished—the mighty offering made — and that "through death our Lord had destroyed him that had the power of death."

Then it was, that even inanimate nature seemed
to sympathise in his struggle. The sun veiled
its face, and darkness covered the land. The
earth reeled to and fro, beneath the earthquake's
shock. And not on the living only did this
day of strange revelations produce its influence.
Even the last resting-places of the dead were
rent asunder, that on the morning of the first
day they too might come forth with their risen
Lord. Then, even the bodies of the slumbering saints started from their graves, and glided
through the city where once they dwelt. Dim
and livid forms, still wearing the cerements of
the tomb — bearing yet its fearful impress — *in*
this breathing world, yet not *of* it — they " appeared to many," as it were, claiming again brotherhood with the living, and teaching them by
their own ghastly presence, the earliest proofs
of a resurrection. Such were the terrors of the
first Good Friday.

Is it strange then, that the members of the
early Church, with awed and chastened spirits,
kept this holy day, and felt that deep indeed
should be their self-abasement at this season of
their Lord's mysterious agonies ? They consid-

ered it as invested with a peculiar solemnity,
and even those who might have been negligent
during the rest of Lent, religiously observed this
day, as the one on which the Bridegroom was
taken from them.[1] And in the same spirit should
we act now. " On this day " — says Bishop Hobart — " all the pursuits of business should be
suspended; the service of the Church devoutly
attended; and the intervals of public worship
devoted to holy meditation on the sufferings of
Christ, and to other pious exercises. By abstinence, self-denial, and humiliation, we should seek
to testify our sympathy in the sufferings of our
Lord, and our lively sorrow for our sins which
occasioned His sufferings. There can be no
greater evidence of insensibility and ingratitude,
than to spend the day sacred to the sufferings
of Christ, in the usual pursuits of business or
pleasure."

Is he then keeping it as he should, who perhaps only escapes from his usual occupation in
the court room or the counting house, for a
single hour to attend the services of the Church ?
Are his thoughts in a proper state for comme-

---

[1] See BINGHAM'S *Orig. Eccles.*, lib. xxi., ch. 1, sec. 1.

morating his Lord's passion, when he passes at
once to the sanctuary from the noise and turmoil
of business, with all its restless and disquieting
cares about him? And has he profited as he
should by these holy services, when he hurries
back at once to the anxieties of this working
world? No — let the merchant desert for the
day, the mart of business — let the professional
man close his office — and the world will begin
to believe, that this is a season holy to the Lord.
Then the words of our Liturgy will come home
to them with power, and sink into their hearts,
and they will realize more deeply the mighty
debt they owe to Him who died for them.

And how beautifully appropriate are all the
services which the Church has prescribed for this
solemn season! The Psalms for the day, composed by David in times of sorrow and distress,
have always been considered as having a still
higher reference to the sufferings and death of
Christ. The *first lesson* for the morning (Gen.
xxii,) by narrating the intended sacrifice of Isaac
on Mount Moriah, points with the voice of prophecy to the coming agonies of the Son of God,
which ages after were to be endured upon the

same spot; while the *second lesson* (John xviii.,)
brings a portion of our Lord's sufferings before
us, in the simple yet touching record of the beloved disciple who was himself a witness. The
first lesson for the evening (Isaiah lii., ver. 13,
and chap. liii.,) contains the most minute and
striking prophecy of the passion of our Lord,
which is to be found in the whole range of the
predictions in the Old Testament, while the
second lesson (Phil. ii.,) contrasts the humiliation
of Christ with His pre-existent dignity, and from
this example inculcates the virtues of unity and
humbleness of mind. Such are the truths which
are now brought before us, and remembering the
inestimable benefits which we have obtained by
this one great sacrifice of our Lord, we can not
but feel that this fast is appropriately named
Good Friday. The recollections which gather
around it may be those of sorrow, yet mingled
with them is the loftiest triumph, for at this
period it was that man's great redemption was
wrought out.

The ordinary themes connected with the sacrifice of our Lord are familiar to all who " profess
and call themselves Christians," and need not be

discussed in a work of this kind. They form the very foundation of all religious teaching. We will therefore endeavor to bring forward one point which is generally less understood — THE WITHDRAWAL OF THE DIVINE PRESENCE FROM THE SUFFERER IN THE HOUR OF HIS GREATEST NEED. And we have selected this from the belief, that it furnishes the most strange feature in all the array of His agony. Overwhelming as were the sorrows which gathered around the Son of Man in the time of His deepest degradation and shame, there were none that can be compared with this. When His death cry—" My God, my God, why hast thou forsaken me ? "—rang in the ears of the astonished spectators, it proclaimed that a new and most bitter ingredient had been added to His cup of misery.

And here we would observe, that we can never fully conceive of the amount of our Lord's sufferings. We have no capacity for comprehending their reality and boundless extent. Our narrow conceptions can never picture to us the unutterable sorrows of an infinite mind. Although of course His Divine nature suffered not, yet its very presence and union with his human nature, endowed the latter with capabilities of agony which no mere mortal could ever possess. Even His boundless knowledge—enabling Him to look forward with certainty to all that was at hand—placed Him in a condition for enduring unspeakable anguish of soul. The wide interval then which separates us from our Lord, necessarily renders our view of all that concerns Him partial and defective. " We see but in part," and of course, " we know but in part." It is one of those subjects of a spiritual nature which we can not grasp. As we are unable to attain to an understanding of the inconceivable bliss which our Lord now inherits, so we can as little explain the depth of agony to which once he sank. Much must be left to humble faith. We must look upon it as a mystery which perhaps in another state of being, with enlarged faculties, may be clear to us.

It is for this reason that we are naturally accustomed to dwell most upon the mere physical and bodily sufferings of our Lord. These we can in some measure imagine. We see the Cross erected before us—the torn and agonized body—the parching thirst—the crown of thorns pressed on the bleeding brow—and the spear thrust into the side. All these things a mere mortal might endure, and they come therefore within the range of our comprehension. But beyond this there is a deeper gulf, into which we seldom send our thoughts forward. The soul also had its sufferings, which we believe no words can ade· quately describe. We gather this from the simple narrative of Scripture. When it speaks of His mental anguish, the writers seem to be aware that all human language is utterly insuffi- cient. How strong therefore are the expressions they select, and what a depth of meaning are they evidently endeavoring to express! Their words signify the greatest possible extremity of sorrow, and anxiety, and distress. " His soul was exceeding sorrowful, even unto death." A dark cloud gathered over Him. His earnest prayer was — " Father, save me from this hour." He seems even deprived of those consolations which good men usually enjoy in the hour of their final struggle, and which enable them to triumph in the prospect of approaching dissolution. But to what can we ascribe this state of despondency to which He was reduced except to the with·

drawal of the Divine Presence, by which God
has promised to uphold His faithful children in
tribulation, and from the enjoyment of which
His own Son was cut off, when " the sorrows of
death compassed Him, and the pains of Hell gat
hold upon Him."

In attempting then to enlarge our knowledge
of this mysterious subject, as far as it has been
revealed by the word of God, we would remark,
*that by the withdrawal of the Divine Presence is
not meant, that the intimate union between the
Divine and human natures was dissolved.* When
on His coming into the world, the Divinity assumed a mortal body, a union was formed which
was indissoluble. It subsisted through all His
toilsome wanderings through Judea, in His want,
and deprivation, and sorrow, and even on the
Cross it did not desert Him. It remained, to
give dignity to His sufferings. It rendered the
victim worthy to be " a propitiation for the sins
of the whole world."[2]   But it was the comfort-

---

[2] Hooker in one place in a single passage puts this point
in a clear light, when referring to some of the ancient
controversies with respect to it. "Theodoret disputeth,
with great earnestness, that 'God' can not be said to

able assurance of its presence which was withdrawn in that fearful hour when most it was
needed.

If however you ask the way in which this was
done, we answer, we can not tell. God has not
revealed to us the manner in which it was effected. He only informs us, that His crucified Son
was for a time deprived of the bright beams
of that Divinity which had taken up its abode
within Him — that while He still continued to
be God as well as man, there was no present
consciousness or feeling of his own perfections.
It seems as if feeble humanity was left for a time
to bear alone, the almost insupportable load
which was crushing it down. Beyond this we
know nothing. We can not explain the way in
which the union of the two natures was at first

suffer. But he thereby meaneth Christ's *Divine Nature*
against Appollinarius, which held even Deity itself pass-
ible. Cyril on the other side against Nestorius as much
contendeth, that whosoever will deny ' very God ' to have
suffered death, doth forsake the faith, which, notwithstanding to hold, were Heresy, if the name of God in this
assertion did not import, as it doth, *the Person of Christ*,
who being verily God, suffered death, but in the flesh, and
not in that substance for which the name of God is given
Him."—*Eccles. Polity*, lib. v., sec. 53.

formed, nor can we fully comprehend the mannei in which the suspension of the Divine Presence took place. We see only its effects, in the mental agony which its departure produced.

The next inquiry then which arises is, with regard to *the reason* of this withdrawal. It was evidently, we think, to place our Lord in a situation which qualified Him for deeper suffering. While the inspirations of the Divinity were burning brightly within Him, He could not drink to its dregs that bitter cup which was put to His lips. There was a consolation and an ineffable bliss of which He must be deprived, that He might be enabled to reach the very extremity of woe.

This is a truth which scarcely needs to be enforced. We know that God is the fountain of all joy and consolation, and the more nearly we are united to Him, the greater is our happiness. " In His presence is fullness of joy, and at His right hand are pleasures for evermore." It is the enjoyment of this bright vision, which imparts such extasy to the saints in glory, and should, even for a single moment, a dark veil be drawn, cutting them off from its contemplation, they would at once droop in sorrow. To our Lord, therefore, mere bodily sufferings, grievous as they were, could have been comparatively but of little moment, had He been animated and upheld by the presence of the Divinity within. But this was not allowed Him, for the grief He was to endure was the accumulation of every sorrow which could be heaped upon Him — so fearful was the ransom to be paid for us. God therefore forsook Him, and He was left in the depth of despondency. Such we believe to be the reason of this mysterious event. It was to qualify our Surety, to bear the whole burden which was to be laid upon Him, and to say, in the words of the ancient prophet—" Behold and see, if there be any sorrow like unto my sorrow, which is done unto me, wherewith the Lord has afflicted me, in the day of His fierce anger."

Again — let us look at this deprivation to our Lord in another respect — *its strangeness.* It was the withdrawal of that which He had ever before possessed. Before the world was, even through the countless ages of the past eternity, His had ever been " the fullness of the Godhead." He had ever shared in all that inexpressible de-

light which must be the attendant of Divinity.
And even when on earth, we have no reason to
suppose, that hitherto its beams had been ob-
scured, or the sensible evidence of its presence
taken away. The Spirit, we are told, was poured
out upon Him " without measure," and we read
in every action which He performed, and in every
word which He spake, the proof that it was done
through the promptings of His Higher nature.
As therefore the *manner* of His existence during
this time is incomprehensible, so also does the
bliss which it afforded Him, transcend our utmost
thoughts. But now, for a season this was taken
away, and the very height of happiness to which
it had always before raised Him, now deepened
the woe, to which by its loss He was reduced,
His feelings could only find utterance in that
plaintive exclamation which was wrung from
Him — " Eli, Eli, lama, sabachthani, that is to
say, My God, My God, why hast thou forsaken
me ! " Yet in this you perceive the strangeness
of the deprivation. He who had been God from
all eternity, now for the first time felt Himself
deserted by the present influence of the Deity.

He felt, that in suffering at least, He was nothing but a man.

But let us illustrate this point by something more within the sphere of our comprehension. Take an angel, who from the moment of his creation, has always rejoiced in the presence of God, and let the light of his Maker's countenance be withdrawn from him. Indescribable would be the wretchedness which in such a case would overwhelm that bright Intelligence, when the beatific vision was removed. Yet we think, that the darkest feature in his sufferings — that which would force him to feel them with the greatest intenseness—would be, the very strangeness of his situation — the fact that it was something which he had never before experienced. Now such, only in an infinitely greater degree, was the case with our Lord. For a brief time, He was left to suffer alone. It was the very climax of His misery — the hour of His deepest humiliation, which was soon however to give place to joy and triumph.

But when he now looks back upon it from His throne of glory, think you, that any thing like regret is felt, for the pain He endured—the fiery

trial through which He passed? No—we know
there cannot be. As the number of the Elect
gather into the Paradise of God, and he' beholds
in these ransomed spirits the prize for which He
contended, widely different emotions must fill His
breast. He sees in them "the travail of His soul,
and is satisfied." He feels no sorrow that He
trod the wine-press of God's wrath. He judges
it worth all His trials and suffering, that He
should lead up many sons and daughters to glory,
and therefore He is contented to have borne all
that He did. He finds an ample recompense in
the sight of the happiness of the redeemed, and
in the glad rejoicings of the unnumbered millions,
who but for His sorrows would have been the
heirs of eternal woe.

Again — we would look at this withdrawal of
the Divine Presence in one other point of view—
the greatness of the sorrow it occasioned. We find
no record of any alleviation afforded our Master
in this hour of intense bitterness. An angel
was indeed sent down, but we are told, it was to
" strengthen Him." Not a word is said about
conferring comfort. It was to endow Him with
the ability to suffer. Now the truth is an obvious

one, that just in proportion to the degree of holiness we have, will be our delight in the presence
of God, and of course, the depth also of distress
we shall feel, when it is withdrawn from us.
The kingly Poet of Israel would exclaim — "My
soul thirsteth for Thee, O God; my flesh longeth
for Thee in a dry and thirsty land, where no
water is." The individual, whose heart has been
sanctified by the Holy Ghost, will feel that the
very existence of his spiritual life depends upon
the continuance of this comfort, and will mourn
its absence in bitterness. How deep then must
have been the sorrow of our Lord, who was
without sin, when this evil befell Him, and He
was no longer cheered by the Divine presence!
We, in the midst of our imperfections and blind-
ness, can never realize the emotions of a Being
of perfect holiness, at such a change. It was the
removal of the sun from the system. It was
condemning Him to darkness and despair.

But there was more than the mere withdrawal
of God's presence. There was also poured out
upon Him, that just retribution of the Almighty,
which was merited by the race whose nature He
had assumed. " He bore our griefs and carried

our sorrows. He was bruised for our iniquities; the chastisement of our peace was upon Him; and with His stripes we are healed. All we like sheep have gone astray; we have turned every one to his own way; and the Lord hath laid upon Him the iniquity of us all." He had placed Himself to endure the punishment of transgressions, which otherwise would have descended upon us, and therefore He was weighed down by the load of divine justice against sin. He stood up to be a Surety, to pay the penalty due from fallen man — to bear the curse and shame — and He suffered them to the uttermost. The very consciousness then of this, must have immeasurably aggravated His anguish, when He felt its most fearful effect — the Almighty, as it were, retiring from Him, and abandoning Him to darkness.

Another necessary consequence of this withdrawal was, that it left Him exposed to the efforts and temptations of the fallen spirits. We find, that when Satan first assaulted Him in the wilderness, he was easily repulsed, for then our Lord was animated with a consciousness of the presence of Divinity, and His communion with

God was uninterrupted. But when this change passed over His soul, and He was forsaken by the Father, then He was left open and exposed to all the arts of the Evil One. The malice and subtlety of that fallen spirit—still powerful even in his apostacy — were exerted to the utmost, and thus literally, " His soul became an offering for sin." It was this which He himself intimated, when He said to His enemies among the Jews—" When I was daily with you in the temple, ye stretched forth no hands against me, but this is your hour, and the power of darkness." As if he had told them — " During the former part of my ministry, I was shielded by divine power. You could effect nothing against me. But now, that aid is withdrawn, and you and the powers of darkness have your hour to tempt and try me. You can wreak your vengeance on my body, and my spiritual enemies on my soul." We can not indeed tell the extent of influence which these apostate spirits are able to exert, but we know that it must be great. And we may well believe that all the strength of our Great Adversary was put forth in his last, decisive struggle with the Son of God. Once he had been foiled, but now the contest was renewed, in the very crisis of this world's fate, when its salvation was on the eve of completion, and all the dearest interests of the countless tribes of man were at stake. We may be sure then, that no weapon which the Great Enemy of our race could wield, was left unemployed. Alone our Redeemer passed through the fiery furnace, "and of the people there was none with Him." Alone He baffled his foes, and wrought out that triumph in which ·through all ages His followers are to share.

Such then we believe is the reason, why this also was added as the most bitter ingredient in the cup of our Master's sorrows — the strangeness of the change to Him — and the greatness of the suffering which it caused. Can not we perceive therefore in this particular, how widely the agonies of our Lord are separated from those which could be endured by any mere mortal? With the early martyrs, the pain was confined to the body. The mind was at peace—nay, more than this — was cheered and elevated by the sensible comforts of the Spirit, so as to be able, even with exultation, to encounter death in its most fearful forms. It was the mortal frame convulsed with agony, but the spirit departing in hope. Yet our Lord was left, desolate and forsaken, and in no other way can we account for the exceeding sorrow which weighed Him down, than by referring it to His agony of mind under that additional affliction of which we have endeavored to speak. We see then, how utterly impossible it is for us to measure the length and breadth of His sufferings, when we compare them with human feelings and affections. There is an unfathomable depth in His mysterious sorrow, which places it far beyond our comprehension. We can no more understand it, than we can the Divine nature. And it was this view of the subject which probably induced the ancient Greek Church to insert among the prayers of its Liturgy, the appropriate petition—" By thine unknown sufferings, O Lord, have mercy upon us."[8]

But yet this consideration should only awaken us to greater gratitude. If His sorrows were infinite, how great the wonder and amazement which should fill our minds, when we remember,

---

[8] Δια των αγνωςων, δου παδηματων, Κυριε ελεηδον ημας.

that they were for us! They were the speaking
and powerful evidences of that "love of Christ,
which passeth knowledge." Let us endeavor
then at present, when the services of the Church
especially calls us to this duty, to meditate upon
these things, until our holiest affections are kindled into exercise, and the voice of praise breaks
forth from our lips. This will be the subject of
our contemplations in that coming world of bliss
to which we trust we are hastening forward.
There, where the treasures of Divine love are
unfolded before us, we shall find in the sufferings
of the Son of God, a theme to which the heart
will ever return with deepened interest as the
ages of eternity roll by. Let us begin then now,
to anticipate the employments of the heavenly
world. We can (to use the beautiful imagery
of Bunyan,) ascend the Delectable Mountains,
and from afar, by the strong eye of faith catch a
glimpse of the portals of the Celestial City, and
as the anthem of its shining inhabitants floats
softly to our ear, strive even now to add our
voices to their glorious melody. We know the
burden of that "new song," and while still in
our earthly state, may familiarize our minds with

it. As the years of our pilgrimage pass away,
and the time of our final retribution draws
nigh, we can learn to meditate with delight upon
that sacrifice, through the unspeakable agonies of
which, we have attained all our hopes of pardon
here and of glory hereafter.

Here then is our trust. Our Lord hath met
the King of Terrors — hath died — hath passed
the portals of the tomb. "Through death He
destroyed him that had the power of death." It
was breaking his sceptre, and depriving him of
all claim to the countless millions who else
would have been his prey. Why then should
human nature shrink back in dread from the
path, over which the Master hath trodden?
Why should we so often stand "shivering on the
brink, afraid to launch away?" Why should
we array the Last Messenger who releases us
from our warfare, with every attribute of terror,
till the heart quails at his approach? Even from
the twilight knowledge of an ancient and heathen
philosophy, we may learn a better lesson. There
he was represented as but the twin brother of
Sleep, as if he only called us to a slumber deeper
and longer than that which each night overtakes

us. There, in the lands in which this mythology prevailed, on many a mouldering tomb is still found the sculptured image of the Angel of Death, and we behold him in the form of a youth his wings folded in repose, and his torch inverted. All is serene, peaceful and beautiful.

Surely then the Christian, to whom all is certainty, may well say, " Death is swallowed up in victory." Trusting in no dim speculations, he " knows in whom he has believed, and that He is able to keep that which he has committed to Him against that day." Standing by the Cross on Calvary, the darkness rolls away from the landscape which stretches out before him, and he sees his path plainly marked. It passes indeed through the wilderness, and down into the dark valley of the Shadow of Death, and over the troubled waters of Jordan, yet he traces it up to the gates of the New Jerusalem — the Eternal City of his God. This then is his hope, which should enable him to greet the Monarch of the Tomb with a calmness which no earthly philosophy could ever give. He realizes that " through the grave and gate of death he shall pass to his glorious resurrection, for His merits, who died, and was buried, and rose again for us, Jesus Christ our Lord."[4]

But yet, all our thoughts are not those of joy and triumph when we dwell on the great Sacrifice. Sorrowful emotions also mingle with them. If every promise of eternal life is bound up in the crucifixion of our Lord, then what must we think of those, who seek no interest in His Redemption? In vain for them were the sufferings—the scourge — the nails — and the Cross — for they have rejected the precious inheritance which thus was purchased for the fallen sons of men. " In vain " did we say? It was more than this. These thrilling scenes will add a deeper horror to their condemnation, for in this manner the means of safety were placed within their reach, but they rejected it, and trampled the blood of the covenant beneath their feet. As they contemplate then the sorrows of our Lord, let them think whether that misery can light, to redeem from which He consented to suffer so fearfully. Let them remember the intensity of His agony, when He uttered the plaintive exclamation —·" My God ! my God ! why hast Thou forsaken me ! "—

[4] *Collect for Easter-Even.*

and the view may awaken them from their death-like apathy.

In a different spirit indeed, this same cry has often been uttered since, by thousands in their dying hour. This bitter lamentation has quivered on the lips of many a sinner, as the shadows of the grave gathered around him. It was not, as with our Lord, the temporary withdrawal of God's favor, but his everlasting departure. He forsook the infatuated mortal who had sinned away his day of grace, that he might reap the retribution his own deeds had worked out. With him, this agonizing cry was the wail of a lost spirit, as its ceaseless woe was commencing. It was quenching the last ray which brightened his path, leaving the desolate immortal to begin the travel of Eternity in darkness and despair.

Thus it is, that from every side of us there comes a voice of entreaty and of warning. Not from the word of God alone—not from the Cross of His Son—are the only incitements to Christians' earnestness to be drawn. The wakeful, spiritual eye may read their solemn appeals in many a scene which meets us as we journey on our daily path. From the parting agonies of each careless wanderer from his Lord, as he enters eternity " not knowing the things which shall befall him there," is heard the startling warning — " Be watchful, O pilgrim through an evil world — gird up thy loins and hasten on- ward—be earnest, be diligent—for the work to be accomplished is great, while the day is passing away, and the shadows of the evening are stretch- ing forward."

EASTER EVEN.

At length the worst is o'er, and Thou art laid
   Deep in thy darksome bed ;
All still and cold beneath yon dreary stone
   Thy sacred form is gone ;
Around those lips where power and mercy hung,
   The dews of death have clung ;
The dull earth o'er Thee, and thy foes around,
Thou sleep'st a silent corse, in funeral fetters wound.

KEBLE'S " Easter Eve."

VI.

EASTER EVEN.

WE have now reached the last of those appropriate services in which the Church calls us to
unite during this solemn Season. When for
weeks we had chastened our souls by fasting and
prayer, that we might be prepared to contemplate the fearful agonies of the Son of God, we
were led by the services of Passion Week to the
Hill of Calvary, and there beheld our Lord expiring on the Cross. But to-day a new scene in
this fearful Tragedy is unfolded before us. The
crucifixion is over — the Son of Man has passed
the gates of Death — His body been pierced by
the soldier's spear, to render it certain that no
life remained — and then the inanimate remains
given by Pilate to Joseph of Arimathea, to be
buried as he would. They have been deposited

in his own new tomb in the garden — the stone
sealed — and the Roman guard placed around it,
" lest His disciples come by night, and steal Him
away." There they are resting, while many are
looking anxiously for the things that should come
after.

Strange indeed must have been " the search-
ings of heart," which took place among those
who thus awaited in trembling expectation, the
further developments of this mystery. With
the disciples it was indeed a day of trouble and
suspense, when conflicting emotions filled their
minds. They scarcely could have known what
to think or believe. Confiding in the Messiah-
ship of their Lord, as they witnessed His oft
repeated miracles, they had " trusted that this
Jesus was He who should have redeemed Israel."
Yet now their lofty hopes, both for themselves
and for their nation, seemed to be interred in His
sepulchre. " Slow of heart," they could not yet
reconcile the facts of His sufferings and His triumph, or learn that the Redeemer was to pass
on to his kingly throne through the furnace of
affliction.

And on Mount Moriah, and even within the

precincts of the Temple, there must also have been anxious and excited hearts. The rites of that Jewish Sabbath were kept as usual—clouds of incense filled the Sanctuary — the smoke of the morning and evening sacrifice rose in the air above the Holy City — and countless thousands of worshippers as heretofore thronged the courts. Yet among those crowds must there not have been many who thought with fear on the deeds of the previous day, and now shuddered at the remembrance of that terrible prayer their own lips had uttered — "His blood be on us and on our children!" Even the priests and rulers must have trembled at the recollection of their own successful violence. They could not forbear to connect His death with the unusual signs which had convulsed all nature. In the very recesses of the Temple, the veil was rent by no mortal hands, and the sacred mysteries of the Holiest exposed to view — a fearful evidence that the Divinity was forsaking His accustomed abode. Did they behold these things without dismay? Did they minister as usual with untroubled minds? Did the former infatuation continue, and the triumph of having removed a rival who led away the people from them, sustain their courage amidst all these mysterious occurrences? We can not believe it. "That Sabbath day was an high day," yet it was no time of festive joy with the rulers of the Jewish nation.

And could we have looked into the spiritual world, and beheld those ranks of fallen angels who carry on a ceaseless warfare against Him, whose praises once they sang with harp and anthem, we believe that there also dismay would have been seen. The long years of temptation and conflict with the Messiah were over, and these His mightiest enemies — to work whose will the Priests and Sadducees were but instruments — had apparently triumphed when they silenced His voice for ever. Yet in this, the moment of seeming victory, must not the Arch-Adversary have felt a consciousness of defeat, as the exclamation, " It is finished," proclaimed to him not only that the sufferings of the Son of God were over, but also that his own sceptre was broken, and the fancied sovereignty forever wrested from his grasp? May not the truth have then first dawned upon a waiting universe, that Christ having " died for our sins," was about to be "raised up again for our justification?" We cannot speak of these things with certainty; yet when we remember the intense interest with which all orders of spiritual beings marked the unfolding of this mighty scheme of redemption, we may well believe that its consummation must have fallen with a crushing weight upon those apostate angels who had been striving to defeat it, and at the same time awakened to its loftiest exercise, the joy and adoration of the myriads who still gathered about the throne.

It is this interval of suspense — this time of doubt and fear among men — when the body of our Lord was still in the tomb, and His soul had gone to "the place of departed spirits" — that is known as Easter Even. It is the Saturday, between the day of the crucifixion, and the morning of Easter Sunday. In the early Church it was kept as a solemn fast, being the only Saturday throughout the year which was thus observed, for even in Lent this day was a festival together with the Lord's day which followed. Thus we find it ordered in the Apostolic Constitutions, as being in accordance with the estab-

lished custom of the Church in that age — "Let
as many as are able, fast on the Friday and Sabbath." (that is Saturday, the Jewish Sabbath,)
"throughout, eating nothing till the cock-crowing in the morning. But if any can not join both
days together in one continued fast, let him however keep the Sabbath a fast, for the Lord speaking of Himself said, 'when the Bridegroom shall
be taken away from them, in those days shall
they fast.'"[1]

The night of this day, (as we learn from the
next chapter of the Apostolic Constitutions,) was
spent as a solemn Vigil, when they assembled
together for the performance of divine service,
reading the Scripture, prayer, and preaching.
There they continued until midnight, and many
even remained until the cock-crowing. "It was
a tradition among the Jews"—says St. Jerome—
"that Christ would come at midnight, as He did
upon the Egyptians at the time of the Passover.
Thence, I think, the Apostolical Custom came,
not to dismiss the people on the Paschal Vigil
before midnight, expecting the coming of Christ;
after which time presuming on security, they keep

[1] *Patres Apos.*, COTEL vol. i., p. 325.

the day a festival."[2] At a later period, when the Church had vanquished the power of ancient Paganism, and begun to put on her robes of power, this Vigil was kept with great pomp. Constantine — as Eusebius tells us, in his life of that emperor — "set up lofty pillars of wax to burn as torches all over the city, and lamps burning in all places, so that the night seemed to outshine the sun at noon-day."

The Church has therefore still continued to command the observance of this day, although the state of society and the forms of life in this age require that the manner in which it is done should be modified.[3] The services which have been provided, are marked by the same wisdom which can be discerned in all the arrangements

[2] BINGHAM's *Orig. Eccles.*, lib. xxi., chap. 1, sec. 32.

[3] The writer has been accustomed for several years, to hold the last Lent service on Easter Even, at 5 P. M., and believes that not one among the week-day services of the Church is better calculated to arrest the attention. That Vesper hour of quiet, when the cares of the busy week are over, in the waning twilight, as the day is softly fading into darkness, seems naturally to harmonize with our feelings of devotion. Then, in solemn meditation we can look back at the services which are gone, and forward to the great Festival of the morrow.

of our venerable Church. In the beautiful Collect for the day, we offer up our humble petitions, "that as we are baptised into the death of our blessed Saviour Jesus Christ, so by continual mortifying our corrupt affections, we may be buried with him; and that through the grave and gate of death we may pass to our joyful resurrection, for His merits, who died and was buried, and rose again for us, Jesus Christ our Lord." The Epistle, from St. Peter, containing that mysterious passage concerning our Lord's "preaching unto the spirits in prison," seems evidently selected by the Church as referring to the condition of His soul during this period; while the Gospel clearly describes His burial, and the care that was taken to "make the sepulchre sure, sealing the stone, and setting a watch."

With the future history of our Lord's body, we are all well acquainted. We know how on the next morning He burst the bands of death, and came forth from the tomb, and then after mingling with His disciples for forty days ascended up visibly into Heaven. But the question, Where was the human soul of our Master during this period? is one which most of His followers are not so well prepared to answer. We reply therefore, it was in the INTERMEDIATE STATE, and to a discussion of this subject we intend to devote the remainder of these pages. We have selected it, because although one most important to us, there is probably no truth asserted in the Creed, which is so little understood.

The faith of the Church then with respect to the doctrine is briefly this — that while the hour of death decides irreversibly the condition of the spirit, so that " they which are holy will be holy still," and for the wicked there will remain no more sacrifice for sin, neither can it be purged away by offering for ever, yet the just do not at once enter into Heaven, nor do the lost descend immediately to their eternal prison. They go to an intermediate state, where they await the last judgment. There indeed the righteous are in happiness, and the wicked in misery, through all the ages which intervene; yet the one can not have " the fullness of joy," nor the other suffer the extremity of their destined misery, until their souls are once more united to their bodies. This takes place at the second coming of our Lord. At that time, the spiritual and earthly parts of our nature will be again brought into union, and the mighty army of the dead gather before the Great White Throne. Then, the Books will be opened—the final sentence be pronounced—the gates of Heaven, and the dreary prison house of the lost, unclose to receive their appointed occupants—and the spirits of all who have ever lived, commence the travel of Eternity.

In endeavoring to state the proofs on which we rest our belief in this doctrine, we naturally turn first to *the inspired word of God*. For, as Lord Bacon has well remarked—" A knowledge of the soul must in the end be bounded by religion, or else it will be subject to deceit and delusion: for as the substance of the soul in the creation was not extracted out of the mass of Heaven and earth by the benediction of a ' producat,' but was immediately inspired by God, so it is not possible that it should be otherwise than by accident, subject to the laws of Heaven and earth, which are the subject of philosophy; and therefore the true knowledge of the nature and state of the soul, must come by the same inspiration that gave the substance."[4]

[4] *Advancement of Learning*. BACON's Works, vol. ii., p. 170, Montague's edit.

We learn then most plainly from Scripture, that the souls of the just do not (as some in all ages have vainly imagined,) sleep with their bodies in utter insensibility, until the morning of the resurrection. Every intimation there given us with regard to our spiritual nature, confirms the truth which reason teaches, that " conscious- ness must be a necessary attribute of a spirit in a disembodied state." Samuel was summoned up from his place of repose, evidently returning reluctantly to the cares of this world, and his inquiry was—" Why hast thou disquieted me, to bring me up!" Every circumstance of the nar- rative too shows, that the spirit of Samuel was truly evoked. Saul evidently believed it, and the sacred penman records it, as if stating an actual occurrence. " And Saul "—says he— " perceived that it was Samuel," and " Samuel said," etc. The son of Sirach also, who is thought to have written two centuries before the Christian era, expresses himself on this topic with the same unhesitating confidence. After giving a brief account of Samuel's life and character, he adds— " And after his death he prophesied and showed the King his end, and lift up his voice from the earth in prophecy, to blot out the wickedness of the people."[5] Josephus too in relating the story, does not betray the slightest suspicion that it was not in truth the soul of Samuel conversing with Saul.[6] We are warranted therefore from this circumstance, not only in drawing an inference that the souls of the departed are in a state of consciousness, but also that this was an article in the popular creed of the Jewish nation. In the same way Moses and Elias appeared on the Mount of Transfiguration, and "talked with our Lord," as being spirits evidently endowed with all those powers which reason teaches us must belong to them.

The same truth is taught by the Apostle Paul, when he asserts—"We are confident, I say, and willing rather to be absent from the body, and to be present," (or conversant) "with the Lord." And again he declares — "For I am in a strait betwixt two, having a desire to depart, and to be with Christ; which is far better." He thus plainly shows us, that the righteous when "absent from the body," are not in a state of insensibility,

[5] *Eccles.* xlvi. 20.
[6] *Antiq.* lib. vi., ch. 15.

but conversant with their Lord — in a situation where they enjoy a degree of communion with Him which they can not have while still in this state of probation. The Apostle did not indeed mean, that at death his spirit should at once pass into that Heaven to which his Lord had ascended, for in another place he speaks of " the crown of righteousness " being " laid up for him," not to be bestowed until that Great Day when his Master should sit as " the righteous Judge," and he should receive it in company with " all them also that love His appearing." " The word ενδημησαι should be rendered "—says Dr. Bloomfield—" not *to be present with*, but (agreeably to the metaphor,) *to be at home with*, implying communion with Him." Even while St. Paul was alive, he was with Christ, and Christ was with him, but the felicity for which he hoped at death was a nearer access to Him, and a greater communication of His favor. He should behold His glory, though not in that full brightness wherein it shall be seen at the day of His final appearing.

This brings us then to the question we would investigate. If the soul is to be in a state of consciousness when it has left the body, whither

does it go? Where is its place of abode? This
inquiry is best answered by considering the circumstances connected with our Lord's death,
since we are to follow in the same path in which
He trod. Whither then did His soul depart?
Can we believe (as Calvin asserted,) that He
went down to the place of torment, and there
endured the pains of a reprobate soul in punishment.[7] The mind shrinks back with horror at
the thought, unsupported as the notion is by any
intimation in Scripture, and directly refuted by
our Lord's own declaration to his penitent companion in suffering. Did His spirit ascend at
once to Heaven, and remain there during the

[7] " It was necessary for him to contend with the powers
of hell and the horror of eternal death . . . .
Therefore it is no wonder, if he be said to have descended
into hell, since he suffered that death which the wrath of
God inflicts on transgressors. . . . . The relation
of those sufferings of Christ, which were visible to men,
is very properly followed by that invisible and incomprehensible vengeance which he suffered from the hand of
God; in order to assure us that not only the body of Christ
was given as the price of our redemption, but that there
was another greater and more excellent ransom, since he
suffered in his soul the dreadful torments of a person condemned and irretrievably lost."—*Institutes, Book* ii., chap.
xvi., sec. 10.

three days which intervened before His resurrection? This could not be, for He afterwards said
explicitly to Mary Magdalene—"Touch me not,
for I am not yet ascended to my Father." He
remained forty days with His disciples upon the
earth, before He departed visibly into Heaven.
The necessary conclusion therefore to which we
must come, is that He went to some place entirely distinct either from the Heaven of rest, or
the prison of final torment. That place was
Paradise, as He declared to the penitent thief—
"To-day shalt thou be with me in Paradise."

What then did the Jews understand by Paradise? We reply—with them it primarily referred to the Garden of Eden, where Adam dwelt
in his state of innocence. But as this was a
type of all·that was pleasant and delightful, they
used the same word also symbolically to repre-
sent that place of happiness in which the just
await their resurrection. "Paradise" — says
Parkhurst — "is in the New Testament, applied
to the state of faithful souls between death and
the resurrection." Hence it was the solemn
good wish of the Jews, (as we learn from the
Talmudists,) concerning a departed friend, "Let

his soul be in the Garden of Eden," or " Let his soul be gathered into the Garden of Eden." And in their prayers for a dying person, they were accustomed to say, " Let him have his por‐ tion in Paradise, and also in the world to come." In this form " Paradise " and " the world to come," are plainly referred to, as being two separate places and states of existence.[8] The same distinction is also made by St. Paul, when in speaking of different visions and revelations he had received, he mentions one in " the third Heaven," and another in " Paradise."[9] Dr. Doddridge, the celebrated Presbyterian divine, in his Family Expositor, thus paraphrases this passage — " Such an one, I say, I did most inti‐ mately know, who was snatched up into the third Heaven, the seat of divine glory and the place where Christ dwelleth at the Father's right hand, having all the celestial principalities and powers in humble subjection to him. . . . . . And I know that having been entertained with these visions of the third Heaven, *on which good men ire to enter after the resurrection*, lest he should

---

[8] Bishop BULL's Works, vol. i., p. 98.

[9] 2 Cor. xii., 4, 6.

be impatient under the delay of his part of the glory there, he was also caught up into Paradise, that garden of God, which is *the seat of happy spirits in the intermediate state, and during their separation from the body.*" To this place then it was that our Lord's spirit went, and there He promised that His suffering companion on the Cross should be also.

> " Where'er thou roam'st, one happy soul, we know,
>   Seen at thy side in woe,
> Waits on Thy triumph — even as all the blest
>   With him and Thee shall rest.
> Each on his cross, by Thee we hang awhile,
>   Watching Thy patient smile,
> Till we have learn'd to say, ''T is justly done,
> Only in glory, Lord, Thy sinful servant own.' "[10]

In the same way, while *Paradise* denotes that portion of the intermediate state which was allotted to the just, there was also a part in which the condemned awaited in misery the coming of the day of doom. This was known by the name of *Tartarus.* The general term for both these places was the Hebrew word *Sheol,* or as it is in the Greek, *Hades,* while the word *Gehenna* was used to signify the place of eternal torments

[10] KEBLE'S *Easter Eve.*

after the resurrection.[11] By translating *Hades* therefore by the English word *Hell* in our Bibles, we often entirely obscure the meaning.[12] Such is the case with that passage in the sixteenth Psalm which refers prophetically to our Lord — " For thou wilt not leave my soul in Hell," (that is in *Hades*, or the intermediate state,) " neither wilt thou suffer thy Holy One to see corruption." This text indeed shows so plainly, that while our Lord's body was in the grave, His soul was in some place called Hades, " that none but an infidel " — saith St. Augustin — " can deny it." It is in Hades that Isaiah has placed that strange

[11] As the object of the writer is to give, if possible, a simple and popular view of this subject, which is so little understood, a critical investigation of the meaning of these words would be out of place in these pages. The reader will find this examination carried out in Bishop Hobart's work on the State of the Departed.

[12] " It is a great pity," — says Wall, (*Hist. Inf. Bap.*, part ii., chap. viii.,)—" that the English translators of the Creed and of the Bible, did not keep the word *Hades* in the translation, as they have done some original words which had no English words answering to them. By translating it *Hell*, and the English having no other word for *Gehenna* (which is the place prepared for the devil and the damned,) than the same word *Hell* likewise, it has created a confusion in the understanding of English readers."

dramatic scene, which is found in the fourteenth chapter of his prophecies. As Homer in the Odyssey (lib. xxiv.) sends the souls of the suitors to Hades, where they meet the spirits of Achilles, Agamemnon, and the other Grecian heroes they had known in life, the Hebrew prophet with the higher inspiration of truth, has given a description which for its inimitable grandeur nothing in the pages of classical antiquity can equal. He shows the proud King of Babylon, after he had been brought to the grave, entering *Sheol*, while the monarchs of the earth who had preceded him to the land of spirits, are poetically represented as rising from their seats at his approach, greeting him with bitter scorn—

" Hades (*Sheol*) from beneath is moved because of thee,
    to meet thee at thy coming:
He roused up for thee the mighty dead, all the great chiefs
    of the Earth:
He maketh to rise up from their thrones, all the kings of
    the nations.
All of them shall accost thee, and shall say unto thee:
Art thou, even thou too, become weak as we?   Art thou
    made like unto us?
Is then thy pride brought down to the grave; the sound
    of thy sprightly instruments?
Is the vermin become thy couch, and the earthworm **thy**
    covering?

How art thou fallen from Heaven, O Lucifer, son of the
    morning?
Art cut down to earth, thou that didst subdue the
    nations?"[18]

It is in Tartarus that the fallen angels also
await their sentence. St. Peter tells us — " God
spared not the angels that sinned, but cast them
down to Hell (*Tartarus*,) and delivered them
into chains of darkness, to be reserved unto judgment." And St. Jude says—" The angels which
kept not their first estate, but left their own
habitation, he hath reserved in everlasting chains
under darkness unto the judgment of the great
day." In Tartarus too was the rich man, while
Lazarus was in Paradise. Dr. Campbell, another
learned Presbyterian divine, and formerly Principal of Marischal College, Aberdeen, says —
" There is no inconsistency in maintaining that
the rich man, though in torment, was not in
Gehenna, but in that part of *Hades* called *Tartarus*, where we have seen already that spirits
reserved for judgment are detained in darkness.
. . . . According to this explication, the rich
man and Lazarus were both in *Hades*, though in

[18] *Bishop* Lowth's *translation.*

very different situations, the latter in the mansions of the happy, and the former in those of the
wretched."[14]

[14] *Prelim. Dis.* vi., part 2. As the charge is often made
against the Church, that she retains this *Popish* doctrine,
we quote occasionally from distinguished Presbyterian
writers, showing that they also have been forced to
acknowledge its truth. On this point, no one is more
explicit than President Dwight of Yale College. In his
system of Theology, (*Sermon* clxiv.) he says—" *There can,
I apprehend, be no reasonable doubt concerning an intermediate state.* St. Peter says of the angels that sinned,
that 'God cast them down to Hell, and delivered them
into chains of darkness, to be reserved unto judgment.'
St. Jude also declares them 'to be reserved,' in like manner, 'unto the judgment of the great day.' From these
declarations it is manifest, that fallen angels have not yet
received their final judgment, nor, of course, their final
reward. This, indeed, seems evident from the phraseology
used by St. Peter, as well as by the declarations of both
him and St. Jude. The word which is rendered from St.
Peter, 'cast them down to Hell,' is in the Greek ταρταρωσας;
literally rendered, 'cast them down to Tartarus.' While
this phraseology plainly declares a place of punishment, it
indicates directly a different state from that, which is
taught by the word γεεννα, (*Gehenna,*) the appropriate
name of *Hell* in the Scriptures. After the rich man died
and was buried, it is said by our Saviour, 'he lifted up his
eyes in Hell, being in torments; in the Greek, εν τω ὁδη,
in Hades ..... The state, in which Lazarus was placed,
is denoted elsewhere by the word *Paradise.* 'To-day,'
said our Saviour to the thief on the cross, 'thou shalt be

The manner in which the general judgment is always mentioned, may well confirm our belief in the doctrine of an intermediate state. When is there to be " rendered to every man according to his works?" When, in other words, is each one to reap his full retribution? Is it the moment he has passed the gates of death and put off this mortal body? This would be by no means in accordance with the declarations of Holy Writ. If we examine its promises, we shall meet with no offer of perfect blessedness which is to be fulfilled before our Lord's second coming. He himself on one occasion declared — "Thou shalt be recompensed" — when? " at the resurrection of the just." The final reward of the righteous is

with me in Paradise.' But we know from our Saviour's own declaration, that when he gave up the ghost on the cross, his spirit went not to Hell, but to *Hades* or *Sheol*. . . . . The thief therefore went to the state which is denoted by this word, and not to that which is denoted by *Heaven*, unless this world is supposed to include Heaven."

We might also bring forward the opinions of distinguished divines of other denominations. For example, John Wesley, the founder of the Methodist Society, avows the doctrine clearly in his *Notes on the New Testament*. See on Luke xxiii., 43. 2 Cor. xii., 4. Rev. i., 18. Rev. xx., 15. So also one of his followers, Dr. Adam Clark. See in his Commentary on Heb. xi., 40. Rev. xv., 13. 14.

always referred to the last day, at "the glorious appearing of the great God, and our Saviour Jesus Christ"—"when Christ who is our life shall appear"—"when the Son of Man shall come in the glory of His Father, with His holy angels." Then it is that He shall recognize His faithful followers before an assembled universe, and receive them to reign with Himself in glory. It is not indeed until the solemn scenes of the judgment are over, that His own chosen Apostles will be admitted to that place, where they shall enjoy in its fullness, the presence of Him in whose footsteps they followed on earth. His declaration was—"I go to prepare a place for you. And if I go and prepare a place for you, I will come again, and receive you unto myself, that where I am there you may be also." But the time of His promised return has not yet arrived. His followers have not yet entered into their final rest, nor will they, until He "comes again to receive them unto Himself."

Still stronger is the inference to be drawn from that declaration of St. Paul—"For this we say unto you by the word of the Lord, that we which are alive and remain unto the coming of

the Lord shall not prevent them which are asleep.
For the Lord himself shall descend from Heaven
with a shout, with the voice of the archangel,
and with the trump of God; and the dead in
Christ shall rise first. Then we, which are alive
and remain, shall be caught up together with
them in the clouds, to meet the Lord in the air:
and so shall we ever be with the Lord."[15] Here
is an explicit account of the order in which each
event shall take place at the last judgment. We
learn from it then, that none have as yet entered
into Heaven. If it were not so, but the just, as
each individual soul passed from the earth, had
gone at once to that place of glory, what meaning would there be in the Apostle's declaration,
that " they which are alive and remain unto the
coming of the Lord shall not prevent," that is,
anticipate, or go into Heaven before, " them that
are asleep," that is, the dead! This assurance
certainly would be useless, if the departed at the
hour of death, had each entered into his final rest.
But the Lord must first descend from Heaven —
then, the dead in Christ shall be raised — then,
those who are at that time living on the earth,

[15] 1 *Thess.* iv., 15, 16, 17.

shall be caught up to meet their Judge — and then the army of the ransomed shall together go in to their reward. "And so," that is, after all these things have taken place, "shall be ever with the Lord." What can be more clear than the order in which these events are here laid down.

In the Apocalyptic Vision, St. John represents the ancient martyrs as resting in the Paradise of God, awaiting their reward until their brethren from the earth have joined them, that together they may enter the celestial city.· " I saw under the altar, the souls of them that were slain for the word of God, and for the testimony which they held: and they cried with a loud voice, saying, How long, O Lord, holy and true, dost thou not avenge our blood on them that dwell on the earth? And white robes were given unto every one of them; and it was said unto them, that they should rest yet for a little season, until their fellow servants also and their brethren, that should be killed as .they were, should be fulfilled."[16] Their happiness was incomplete. They are "under the altar" — not in the full presence

[16] *Rev.* vi., 9, 10, 11.

of God, but in a safe and holy place. Their portion is not yet that of perfect bliss, but only of
tranquility and peace. They are not serving God
actively, as do the angels, but are at rest, awaiting their call to judgment and to Heaven. Anxiously do they look forward to the day which is
to introduce them into the joy of their Lord, and
therefore their inquiry is, " How long, O Lord,
holy and true?" But they are told, that they
must " rest yet for a little season," until the circle
of the martyrs is completed, and the number of
the elect gathered in; that thus, in the harvest
time of the earth, all who had suffered in the
great cause of man's redemption — the sowers
and the reapers in the world's wide field—might
all rejoice together. Yet in the meanwhile, to
comfort them in this state of expectation, and as
some little earnest of the promise, " white robes
were given unto every one of them."[17]

It is singular, that exactly the same idea is
given in the Apocryphal Book of Esdras, where
after the writer had made inquiry of the angel
with regard to the mysteries of the world to
come, he receives this reply—" Did not the souls

[17] See NEWMAN'S Sermon on this passage, vol. iii., p. 399.

also of the righteous ask question of these things
in their chambers, saying, How long shall I hope
on this fashion? When cometh the fruit of the
floor of our reward? And unto these things
Uriel the archangel gave them answer, and said,
Even when the number of seeds is filled in you"
—that is, when the number of the elect is accomplished.[18]

[13] *Esdras*, iv., 35, 36. Dr. Macknight, another celebrated Presbyterian divine, supports the same views.
For instance, in his commentary on Heb. xi., 39, 40, he
says—"The Apostle's doctrine, *that believers are all to be
rewarded together and at the same time*, is agreeable to
Christ's declaration, who told His disciples that they were
not to come to the place He was going away to prepare
for them, till He returned from Heaven to carry them to
it (John xiv., 3.) Further, that the righteous are not to
be rewarded till the end of the world, is evident from
Christ's words (Matt. xiii., 40, 43.) In like manner St.
Peter hath told us, that the righteous are to be made glad
with their reward at the revelation of Christ (1 Pet. iv.,
13.) John also tells us, that when He shall appear, we
shall be made like Him, for we shall see Him as He is
(1 John iii., 2.) *This determination, not to reward the
ancients without us, is highly proper*, because the power
and veracity of God will be more illustriously displayed in
the view of angels and men, by raising the whole of Abraham's seed from the dead at once, and *by introducing
them into the heavenly country in a body, after the public
acquittal at the judgment; than if each were made perfect
separately at their death.*"

Another strong proof from Scripture is found in that mysterious declaration of St. Peter, with regard to our Lord—" Being put to death in the flesh, but quickened by the Spirit; by which also He went and preached unto the spirits in prison, which sometime were disobedient, when once the long suffering of God waited in the days of Noah." Many attempts have been made to explain away this text, yet when carefully analyzed, its natural rendering seems to present a full confirmation of the doctrine of an intermediate state. The most masterly discussion of it is given by Bishop Horsley,[19] where he proves conclusively, that in its interpretation by the ancient Church, it was always referred to the descent of our Lord into the place of departed spirits. Let us then as briefly as possible follow his train of reasoning in the explanation of this verse.

The meaning of the whole passage turns upon the interpretation we give to the words " spirits in prison." " The invisible mansion of departed spirits " — says Bishop Horsley — " though certainly not a place of penal confinement to the good, is nevertheless in some respects a prison.

[19] HORSLEY'S Sermons, vol. ii., p. 86, Serm. xx.

It is a place of seclusion from the external world, a place of unfinished happiness, consisting in rest, security, and hope, rather than enjoyment. It is a place which the souls of men never would have entered, had not sin introduced death, and from which there is no exit by any natural means for those who have once entered. The deliverance of the saints from it is to be effected by our Lord's power. As a place of confinement, therefore, though not of punishment, it may well be called a prison. The original word however in this text imports not of necessity so much as this but merely a place of safe keeping: for so this passage might be rendered with great exactness. *He went and preached to the spirits in safe keeping.* And the invisible mansion of departed spirits is to the righteous a place of safe keeping, where they are preserved under the shadow of God's right hand, as their condition sometimes is described in Scripture, till the season shall arrive for their advancement to future glory; as the souls of the wicked, on the other hand, are reserved in the other division of the same place, unto the judgment of the great day. Now if Christ went and preached to souls of men thus

in prison, or in safe keeping, surely He went to
the prison of those souls, or to the place of their
custody; and what place that should be but the
Hell of the Apostles' Creed, to which our Lord
descended, I have not met with the critic that
could explain. The souls in custody, or in prison,
to whom our Saviour went in His disembodied
soul and preached, were those which *formerly
were disobedient.* The expression *formerly* were,
or *one while* had been disobedient, implies, that
they were recovered from that disobedience, and,
before their death, had been brought to repentance and faith in the Redeemer to come. To
such souls He went and preached."

The meaning of the sentence, " being put to
death in the flesh, but quickened by the Spirit,"
must also claim our attention. The word " Spirit,"
is here used in antithesis to the one translated
" flesh." If therefore the latter refers, as it necessarily does, to that part of our Lord's nature
on which alone death could take effect, that is,
his body; the former must refer to that part over
which the Destroyer had no power, that is, his
soul. And as the word " quickened " is often
used to signify, not merely a restoration of life

which has been extinguished, but the preservation of life which then subsists, the Apostle's
words may be well rendered — " Being put to
death in the flesh, but quick in the Spirit," that
is, surviving in His soul the stroke of death which
His body had sustained, " by which," or rather
" in which," that is, in which surviving soul, " he
went and preached to the souls of men in safe
keeping." Such is the rendering given by Mr.
Polwhele in his *Essay on the State of the Soul
after Death.* " The original words " — he says
— " are very strong and decisive. Literally signifying, ' dead in His body ' — ' lighted up with
new life in His soul.' Escaped from the burden
of His mortal body, His soul was animated with
a more ardent vivacity — was rendered capable
of more powerful energies, and with a life thus
kindled into a brighter flame, He went and
preached to the spirits whose bodies had perished
in the deluge."

Another point with reference to this text remains to be inquired into — why are the ante-
diluvians especially mentioned as being those to
whom this preaching was addressed ? Were not
the souls of all who since their day had died in

penitence, equally interested in our Lord's message? "To this I can only answer"—says
Bishop Horsley—"that I think I have observed,
in some parts of Scripture, an anxiety, if the expression may be allowed, of the sacred writers
to convey distinct intimations that the antedilu-
vian race is not uninterested in the redemption
and the final retribution. . . . . It may be
conceived, that the souls of those who died in the
dreadful visitation of the deluge might from that
circumstance have peculiar apprehensions of themselves, as the marked victims of divine vengeance,
and might peculiarly need the consolation which
the preaching of our Lord in the subterranean
regions afforded to these prisoners of hope."

Did He then publish those lofty doctrines of
the Gospel, which now form the themes of His
earthly ministers—the obligation of repentance
and faith, by which the children of this world
are summoned to their Lord? We answer, no—
for He was not offering a new period of probation to the generation which died "in the days
of Noah." Their condition for Eternity was settled, when the rushing flood overwhelmed them
and they perished amid the ruins of the Elder

world. Yet might He not have proclaimed to those, who having died in penitence, had been thus waiting and watching for ages, that at length the mighty sacrifice was offered up — that He had finished the work of redemption — and was now going to plead as their Intercessor before His Father's throne? Might He not thus give assurance to the hope, to which for so long a time they had been cleaving? We see nothing improbable in the idea.

Such then is the analysis and rendering of this passage, in which the most celebrated divines agree. If they have interpreted it aright, it proves most conclusively the fact of the descent into Hades. And through many ages of the Church, this text was relied upon as a principal foundation of this Catholic doctrine. St. Austin is stated to have been the first writer who ventured to doubt that this was the literal sense of St. Peter's declaration. In the Articles of Religion adopted at the Convention held in 1552, the sixth year of Edward VI., and published by the King's authority in the following year, the third article is in these words—" As Christ died and was buried for us, so also it is to be believed

that He went down into Hell; for the body lay
in the sepulchre until the resurrection, but His
ghost departing from Him, was with the ghosts
that were in prison, or in Hell, as the place of St.
Peter doth testify." When however, ten years
later, in the fifth year of Queen Elizabeth, the
Thirty-nine Articles were adopted in their present
form, while Christ's descent into Hell was still
asserted, the proof of it from this text of St. Peter
was omitted.[20] We think however, that the
Church by setting forth this passage in the Epistle for Easter Even, seems to imply that it should
be rendered as referring to our Lord's soul, particularly as it is followed by the Gospel, which
describes so clearly the condition of the other
part of His nature.

We will present one more passage from Scripture. In Rev. xx., 13, 14, we find this description
given of the conclusion of all things earthly—
the final triumph of the human race over death—
and the abandonment forever of the intermediate
state. " And Death and Hell (*Hades*) delivered
up the dead which were in them; and they were
judged every man according to their works.

[20] Bishop HORSELEY, vol. ii., p. 99 .

And Death and Hell (*Hades*) were cast into the lake of fire. This is the second death." By this sublime personification it is clearly stated, that Death shall deliver up the bodies, and Hades the spirits which were subject to their dominion, and that then the latter shall be destroyed. Dr Thos. Scott in his Commentary, thus paraphrased this passage — " The grave, and separate state, will give up the bodies and souls contained in them, so that the whole multitude, which shall have lived upon earth . . . . . . shall experience a reunion of their souls with their bodies. Then Death and Hell, the grave and the separate state (represented as two persons,) will ' be cast into the lake of fire ;' that is, they shall subsist no longer, to receive the bodies and souls of men ; there shall be no death in Heaven ; and all the wicked will be cast into the place of torment, in which death and the separate state will be swallowed up: for ' this is the second death,' the final separation of sinners from God, without hopes of being restored to His favor, or delivered from His wrath." Dr. Campbell (the same Presbyterian divine from whom we have already quoted,) thus renders it — " The death which consists in

the separation of the soul from the body, and
the state of souls intervening between death and
judgment shall be no more. To the wicked, these
shall be succeeded by a more terrible death, the
second death, the damnation of Gehenna, *Hell*
properly so called. Indeed, in this sacred book,
the commencement, as well as the destruction of
this intermediate state, are so clearly marked, as
to render it impossible to mistake them. In
chap. vi., 8, we learn that *Hades* follows close at
the heels of death. 'And I looked, and behold,
a pale horse, and his name that sat on him was
Death, and Hell (*Hades*) followed with him.'
From this passage, in chap. xx., we learn also, that
both are involved in one common ruin at the universal judgment."

Such is a brief statement of the Scripture argument for this doctrine. We now pass on to the
consideration, *that it has always, even from Primitive Times, been an Article of Faith in the
Catholic Church.* The learned Bingham explicitly declares it to have been the belief of the
early Church, that " the soul is but in an imperfect state of happiness till the Resurrection,
when the whole man shall obtain a complete

victory over death, and by the last judgment be established in an endless state of consummate happiness and glory."[21]

St. Clement, of whom the Apostle Paul speaks as his "fellow laborer, whose name is in the Book of Life," thus writes in his Epistle to the Corinthians — " All the generations from Adam to this day are past and gone, but they that have finished their course in charity, according to the grace of Christ, possess the region of the godly, who shall be manifested in the visitation of the kingdom of Christ. For it is written, 'Enter into thy chambers, for a very little while, till my wrath and fury be passed over, and I will remember the good day, and will raise you again out of your graves.'"[22]

Justin Martyr, who lived about the middle of the second century, in his dialogue with Trypho, among the Catholic doctrines taught him when he first became a Christian, delivers this for one — " That the souls of the godly, (after death till the resurrection,) remain in a certain better region, and unrighteous and wicked souls in an

[21] *Orig. Eccles.*, lib. xv., chap. 3, sec. 16.
[22] *Patres Apos. Cotel.*, vol. i., p. 276.

evil one." And in the very same book he con-
demns as an error in the Gnostics, their holding
the belief—" That as soon as they die, their souls
are received up into Heaven."[23]

Similar to this is the testimony of Irenæus,
who lived also in the second century. In argu-
ing against some ancient heretics, who held,
that when they died their souls went at once to
Heaven, he urges against them the example of
our Saviour, " who," says he, " observed in Himself the law of dead persons, and did not presently after His death go to Heaven, but stayed
three days in the place of the dead. . . . .
Whereas then our Lord went into the midst of
the shadow of death, where the souls of deceased
persons abode, and then afterwards rose again in
the body, and was after his resurrection taken
up to Heaven, it is plain that the souls of His
disciples, for whose sake the Lord did these things,
shall go likewise to that invisible place appointed
to them by God, and there abide till the resurrection, waiting for the time thereof; and afterward
receiving their bodies, and rising again perfectly,
i. e. in their bodies as our Lord did, shall so

[23] Bishop BULL, vol. i., p. 110.

come to the sight of God."[24]   Again, in his fifth
Book, he expressly distinguishes Paradise from
the Kingdom of Heaven, and reckons it a lower
degree of happiness " to enjoy the delights of
Paradise," than " to be counted worthy to dwell
in Heaven."   But yet he acknowledges that the
Saviour shall be seen in both, " according as they
shall be worthy or meet who see Him."   And he
concludes the chapter with the declaration, " that
those that are saved shall proceed by degrees to
their perfect beatitude."   That is, that they shall,
as St. Ambrose says, " through the refreshments
of Paradise, arrive at the full glories of the Heavenly kingdom."[25]

Tertullian, who lived at the close of the second
century, calls Paradise, " a place of divine plea-
santness, appointed to receive the spirits of the
saints."[26]   He says also, " Heaven is not yet open
to any, the earth, or Hell, being yet shut, but
that at the end of the world, the Kingdom of
Heaven shall be unlocked."   Again—" All souls
are in Hell (*Hades*,) that there are both punish·

---

[24] WALL on *Inf. Bap.*, part ii., chap. 8.
[25] Bishop BULL, pp. 111, 112.
[26] Ibid. p. 112.

ments and rewards, that both Dives and Lazarus
are there, that the soul is both punished and
comforted in Hell (*Hades*,) in expectation of the
future judgment."[27] And even after he had fallen
into the heresy of the Montanists, he was obliged
to admit this to be a Catholic doctrine, " that
the good souls in that subterranean region, do
enjoy a happiness not to be despised, that they
do in the bosom of Abraham receive the comfort
of the Resurrection to come, that is, that they
are at present in a state of rest and happiness,
and live in a sure and certain hope of a greater
happiness at the resurrection."[28]

In the same way, the author of Questions and
Answers to the Orthodox, (who is supposed to
have lived in the fourth century,) in his reply to
the seventy-fifth question, having said that in this
life there is no difference as to worldly concerns,
between the righteous and the wicked, immediately adds — " But after death, presently the
righteous are separated from the unrighteous.
For they are carried by angels into their meet
places. And the souls of the righteous are con-

---

[27] Lord KING's *Hist. of Apos. Creed*, p. 114.
[28] Bishop Bull, p. 113.

veyed into Paradise, where they enjoy the conversation and sight of Angels and Archangels,
and of our Saviour Christ also by way of vision:
according to what is said, when we are absent
from the body, we are present with the Lord.
But the souls of the unrighteous are carried to
the infernal regions, &c. And they, (that is,
both sorts of souls,) are kept in their meet places
till the day of the Resurrection and recompense."[29]

Novatian, in the third century, says—" Those
places which lie under the earth, are not empty
of distinguished and ordered powers; for that is
the place whither the souls both of the godly
and ungodly are led, receiving the forejudgment
of their future doom." Lactantius, of the same
century, says — " None should think, that souls
were immediately judged after death; for they
are all detained in one common custody, till the
time shall come when the greatest Judge shall
examine their respective merits." Hilary, in the
middle of the fourth century, says — " It is the
necessary law of nature, that bodies should be
buried, and that souls should descend into hell,

[29] Bishop BULL, p. 123.

where they are reserved for an entrance into the
Heavenly kingdom by the custody of the Lord,
to wit, in the bosom of Abraham, unto which a
great gulf hinders the wicked from approaching."[30] Such indeed is the uniform testimony of
the Fathers of the early Church. They believed
not that the departed had already entered into
the perfect bliss of Heaven, but, (in the words of
St. Chrysostom,) "that they will not be crowned
before us, God having appointed one time of cor-
onation for all."

On this doctrine also were founded those
Commendatory Prayers for the dead, which were
used in the ancient Liturgies. These, known by
the names of St. Peter's, St. James's, St. Mark's,
(or St. Cyril's,) and St. John's Liturgy, were
used in the Oriental Churches, and, as has been
shown by Mr. Palmer, in his Antiquities of the
English Ritual, are undoubtedly the four original
forms from which all the Liturgies in the world
have been taken. "They resemble one another
too much to have grown up independently, and
too little to have been copied from one another."

[30] Quoted in Lord KING's *Hist. of Apos. Creed*, p. 214-
215-216.

One point of correspondence is, that each of them has a prayer in the Communion Service, " for the peace of all those who have departed this life in God's faith and fear," concluding with a petition for communion with them. A portion of this prayer was in these words—"We commend unto Thy mercy, O Lord, all other Thy servants, which are departed hence from us with the sign of faith, and now do rest in the sleep of peace: grant unto them, we beseech Thee, Thy mercy and everlasting peace ; and that at the day of the general resurrection, we, and all they which be of the mystical body of Thy Son, may altogether be set at His right hand, and hear that His most joyful voice, ' Come unto me, O ye that be blessed of My Father, and possess the kingdom which is prepared for you from the beginning of the world.' Grant this, O Father, for Jesus Christ's sake, our only Mediator and Advocate." This prayer was retained in the Liturgy in " Edward VI.'s 1st Book," but altered in the 2d, at the instigations of Bucer and Calvin. This was pro- bably done, as Mr. Palmer conjectures, because these prayers were so connected in the minds of the common people with the idea of purgatory, that their continuance would have involved the risk of propagating this pernicious error. As remodeled, the prayer in our service now stands thus—"And we also bless Thy holy name for all Thy servants departed this life in Thy faith and fear, beseeching Thee to give us grace to follow their good examples, that with them we may be partakers of Thy heavenly kingdom.

We do not pretend to discuss the propriety of these prayers; we only mention their existence in the ancient Liturgies, as furnishing a proof of the belief of the Church in the state of Paradise after death. " This custom "—said the learned Bishop Collier—" seems to have gone on the principle that supreme happiness is not to be expected till the resurrection; and that the interval between death and the end of the world, is a state of imperfect bliss."[31]

Thus it is then that the Church has inherited this truth, and so she has retained it. Her third Article is—" As Christ died for us, and was buried, so also it is to be believed, that He went down into Hell;" while in her creed she teaches

[31] *Eccles. Hist. of Great Britain*, Part II., Book IV., p 257.

her children ever to confess — " He descended into Hell;" inserting in the margin by way of explanation, " He went into the place of departed spirits." In the same way she recognizes the doctrine of the intermediate state in all her public offices. She never speaks of the fullness of joy as something to be attained by the Christian immediately after death, but looks forward to it with hope, as a consummation to follow the second coming of our Lord, the resurrection of the dead, and the judgment of the last day. Thus in the collect for the first Sunday in Advent, we pray, that " when Christ shall come again in His glorious majesty to judge both the quick and dead, we may rise to the life immortal."

In the Burial Service, as we might naturally expect, we find a plain distinction made between the rest we are to inherit at death, and that which is to be our portion at the last day. For instance, in one of the concluding prayers, we entreat the Father, " that when we shall depart this life, we may rest in Him; and that at the general resurrection in the last day, we may be found acceptable in His sight, and receive that blessing which His well beloved Son shall then

pronounce to those who love and fear Him, saying, Come, ye blessed children of my Father,
receive the kingdom prepared for you from the
beginning of the world." Here, two separate
times and two distinct rewards are mentioned..
In the same way, in one of the other prayers,
after speaking of " those who have finished their
course in faith," as " now resting from their
labors," we are taught to look forward to a still
higher stage of felicity to which they may reach,
and therefore pray — " And we beseech Thee,
that we, with all those who are departed in the
true faith of Thy holy name, may have our perfect consummation and bliss, both in body and
soul, in Thy eternal and everlasting glory."[32]

Again — another argument in support of this
doctrine is derived from *its being so evidently in
accordance with reason.* A belief indeed in the
immediate entrance of the soul into its full reward

---

[32] This prayer in the service of the Church of England
is even more explicit, where the petition is offered to God,
" of His gracious goodness shortly to accomplish the number of His elect, and to hasten His kingdom : that we, with
all those that are departed in the true faith of His holy
name, may have our perfect consummation and bliss both
in body and soul."

or punishment is one which necessarily leads us
into inextricable difficulties.

Each individual passes through his probation
here, a compound being, the earthly and the
spiritual united by a chain, the links of which we
can not discover, though we daily and hourly
feel the influence of one part of our nature upon
the other. The material and the immaterial sin
and suffer together. Tempting and being tempted, they go through life—the spirit by its imaginings urging on its sluggish partner to action,
while the body by the outward sense trammels
down the soul, to become " of the earth, earthly."
Participating in the same acts, and deserving of
the same recompense, should they not be united
before they fully enter on that state of bliss or
woe which is to be unchanged through eternity?
Can we indeed conceive of any retribution which
will fitly reward man for all his doings here, if it
does not act upon both parts of his nature? Can
he fully rejoice or suffer, while existing as a purely
spiritual being, in this state of separation? Can
we believe therefore that he will receive his final
sentence — or that there will be any use in pro-
nouncing it — until he stands before the throne,

the same he was in every respect, while living a
probationer here? Why then should he enter
into his final state before that hour arrives?

Again — supposing that he does pass at once
into Heaven or Hell, judgment in that case must
be pronounced upon him as soon as his spirit
leaves the body. Must not then the process of
finally acquitting or condemning the disembodied
souls which each hour are winging their flight to
the eternal world, be ceaselessly going on? This
would indeed entirely set aside the general judgment of the last day, unless we can suppose the
absurdity, that now the spirit is judged, but then
the body alone will stand up for retribution.
For what could it be but an empty show, to
recall from Heaven the countless tribes of the
just after they have been glorified there for ages,
and then once more to return them to that abode,
with the sentence, " Enter ye into the joy of your
Lord ! " Bishop Sherlock, in his " Practical Dis-
course concerning a Future Judgment," sums up
this argument in a single sentence — " And the
truth is, if all men have a final sentence passed
on them as soon as they go into the other world,
it is very unaccountable, why Christ at the last

day shall come with such a terrible pomp and solemnity to judge and *condemn* those, who are judged, and condemned, and *executed* already as much as they can ever be." But the plain teaching of Scripture is, that there should be a day at the end of the world, when not only the unnumbered multitudes of the human race, but also the apostate angels who are " reserved in chains" against that solemn hour, shall together receive the sentence which all eternity can not reverse.. Our Lord is now represented, standing as Mediator before the throne of His Father, and not until the mighty drama of this world is entirely concluded, will He ascend the tribunal of judgment.

Neither, on the other hand, can it be argued, that this admission to a state of rest merely and imperfect bliss, would in any way forestall the judgment of the last day, or that the solemnities of Christ's tribunal would be rendered vain by that previous knowledge of our destiny, which must be gained from our intermediate state. " The condition of one who dies in his sins, and awakes to a sense of the retribution that awaits him, may, not inaptly, be compared to that of a

criminal who is committed to a gaol for trial,
without the slightest hope of escaping conviction.
It could hardly be said of such a person, that his
fear and anguish there would forestall the solemnities of justice, and render nugatory the subse-
quent administration and execution of the law.
The forms and proceedings of earthly justice do
not indeed, provide a precisely similar illustration
to the case of those who have persevered in well
doing; but nevertheless, we are unable to comprehend, why the analogy should not likewise be
extended to them. What is there unreasonable
in the surmise, that a righteous man may awaken
from death to that full assurance of acquittal and
acceptance which some have affirmed to be at-
tainable even in the present life? Why may he
not be placed in a state of which the enjoyment
shall consist in the knowledge that his trials and
agitations are at an end, that the forgiveness of
his sins is finally sealed, and that a reward will
at some period be assigned him, proportioned to
his faithfulness, by the infallible wisdom and
goodness of his Judge?"[88]

How natural then seems the order of events,

[88] *British Critic*, No. 17.

when we adopt the belief of an intermediate state! New light is thus poured upon many a passage of Scripture, while every difficulty which was suggested by the reason, at once passes away. There we behold the departed, resting in their separate mansions, through all the ages which intervene between the hour of death and the final consummation of all things. In peace the just repose, for the cares and sorrows of this lower world have passed away for ever, and in the full assurance of hope they look forward to that hour, when their " Lord shall be revealed from Heaven," and they be admitted to the fullness of joy, in the " place which he hath prepared for them." There also, yet separated by " a gulf which they can not pass,"[34] are the wicked. The record of a wasted life is ever before them, for already conscience has commenced her work, and they feel the gnawings of that worm which dieth not for ever. In trembling and fear therefore, they await the revolution of that cycle of ages, and the coming of that day of decision, when they shall be forced to descend to a deeper, more awful state of torment. Thus it is, that the

[34] *Luke*, xvi., 26.

general judgment becomes, as Scripture repre
sents it, the winding up of this world's history
There, the descendants of Adam, of "every kin
dred, and tongue, and people, and nation," meet
for the last time — they are "judged for their
works"—the final separation is made—and they
pass away, to begin their endless retribution.[85]

A single question more remains to be answered.

[85] It will be at once perceived, that this doctrine is
widely different from the belief of the Romanists in Purgatory. Their doctrine is, (as given in their own words)
—" Some there are, though I fear but few, that have
before their death so fully cleared all accounts with the
Divine Majesty, and washed away all their stains in the
blood of the Lamb, as to go straight to Heaven after
death; and such as those stand not in need of our prayers.
Others there are, and their numbers are very great, who
die in the guilt of deadly sin, and such as these go straight
to Hell, like the rich glutton in the Gospel, St. Luke, xvi.,
and therefore cannot be bettered by our prayers. But
besides these two kinds, there are many Christians, who,
when they die, are neither so perfectly pure and clean, as
to exempt them from the least spot or stain, nor yet so
unhappy as to die under the guilt of unrepented deadly
sin. Now such as these the Church believes to be, for a
time, in a middle state, which we call Purgatory; and
these are they who are capable of receiving benefit by our
prayers."—*The Catholic Christian Instructed. By the
Most Rev. Dr.* CHALLONER.

It is the inquiry, *What was the object of our Lord's descent into the place of departed Spirits?* ·

One end answered by it was, *that in this respect also He conformed Himself to the lot of those whose nature He had assumed.* When He left "the glory which He had with the Father before the world was," it seems to have been His purpose to become "like unto us in all things, sin only excepted." He passed through every trial to which frail humanity is subjected. His were the feebleness and pains of wailing infancy—the cares which gather around the years of manhood—the shrinking of nature at the sight of death—and the last convulsive struggle which bursts the prison-house of clay. And even when He entered the gates of the grave, He continued to tread the same path in which each one of us—His brethren after the flesh — must one day walk. His body was committed to the tomb, after a time to be awakened again as an incorruptible and spiritual body, freed from all human infirmities, and then to pass into the Heavens. And for the same reason must His soul also abide in the resting place of those He came to redeem, until the hour in which it was to be once more united with His body. Thus it was, that the humiliation of the Son of God was not confined to this world. It did not end with the agonies of the Crucifixion. It continued even after he had passed the veil which separates the living from the dead. As a disembodied spirit, He found that He must still acknowledge brotherhood with mortals from the earth.

Again — *our Lord thus proved to us the certainty of our victory over Hades.* We point to the resurrection, and say, " Thus it is that we know we also shall triumph over the grave. He hath burst the band of death asunder, and with the like power shall His people also be gifted." This it is, which sheds a glory around the tomb, and lights up its gloomy caverns with a celestial radiance.

But would not the work have been incomplete, if no pledge had been given us of the Spirit's victory in the invisible world—if our Master had neglected to point out the path it also was to tread, in the interval between " death and the resurrection ? " But " He hath done all things well." Nothing was left unaccomplished. His grace was displayed even in the mansions of the departed, and to us therefore they are divested of all ter-

ror. "His soul was not left in Hades," neither
shall His children be forever detained there. He
now " has the keys of Hell (*Hades*) and of Death,"
and shall release them when the appointed hour
comes, that they too may ascend as He did, to
the " fullness of joy."

And may we not add also, that another object
of His descent was, *that He might there proclaim
the news of His redemption to the spirits which
were in safe keeping?* We have already alluded
to this, when discussing that difficult passage in
St. Peter, and stated what must have been the
manner of His preaching. There, the righteous
had rested for ages, in anticipation of that future
atonement which was to be wrought out by the
Son of God. Is there any thing strange then in
the idea, that when that ransom had been paid,
which secured their salvation, and the power of
their great Enemy was forever broken, He should
descend and unfold these glorious tidings to the
countless myriads of the redeemed? While on
earth, they had looked forward with the anticipation of hope, and " rejoiced to see that day "
even through the mist of intervening centuries;

but now, these visions were realized and the Messiah Himself proclaims, that "it is finished."

"The passage in St. Peter, which speaks of Christ as having 'preached to the spirits,' gives, we think"—says an eloquent living writer—"something of foundation to the opinion, that whilst His body was in in the sepulchre, Christ preached to spirits in the separate state, opening up to them, probably, those mysteries of redemption into which even angels, before-time, had vainly striven to look. The kings, and the prophets, and the righteous men, who had desired to see the things which appostles saw, and had not seen them, and hear the things which they heard, and had not heard them—unto these, it may be, Christ brought a glorious roll of intelligence; and we can imagine Him standing in the midst of a multitude which no man can number, who had all gone down to the chambers of death with but indistinct and far-off glimpses of the promised Messiah, and explained to the eager assembly the beauty, and the stability of that deliverance which He had just wrought out through obedience and blood-shedding. And, oh, there must then have gone forth a tide of the

very loftiest gladness through the listening crowds
of the separate state; and then, perhaps, for the
first time, admiration and extacy summoning out
the music, was heard that anthem, whose rich
peal rolls down the coming eternity, 'Worthy,
worthy, worthy is the Lamb.' Then, it may be,
for the first time, did Adam embrace all the mag-
nificence of the promise, that 'the seed of the
woman should bruise the serpent's head;' and
Abraham understand how the well-being of the
human population depended on one that should
spring from his own loins; and David ascertain
all the meaning of mysterious strains, which, as
prefiguring Messiah, he had swept from the harp-
strings. Then too, the long train of Aaron's
line, who had stood at the altar, and slain the
victims, and burnt the incense, almost weighed
down by a ritual, the import of whose ceremonies was but indistinctly made known—then, it
may be, they were suddenly and sublimely taught
the power of every figure, and the expression of
every rite; whilst the noble company of prophets,
holy men who 'spake as they were moved by the
Holy Ghost,' but who, rapt into the future, uttered
much which only the future could develop—these,

as though starting from the sleep of ages, sprang into the centre of that gorgeous panorama of truth which they had been commissioned to outline, but over whose spreadings there had rested the cloud and the mist; and Isaiah thrilled at the glories of his own saying, 'unto us a child is born, unto us a son is given;' and Hosea grasped all the mightiness of the declaration, which he had poured forth whilst denouncing the apostacies of Samaria, 'O Death, I will be thy plagues; O Grave, I will be thy destruction.'

"We know not why it may not thus be considered that the day of Christ's entrance into the separate state was, like the Pentecostal day to the Church upon earth, a day of the rolling off of obscurity from the plan of redemption, and of showing how 'glory, honor and immortality,' were made accessible to the remotest of the world's families; a day on which a thousand types gave place to realities and a thousand predictions leaped into fulfillment; a day therefore, on which there circulated through the enormous gatherings of Adam and his elect posterity, already ushered into rest, a gladness which had never yet been reached in all the depth of their beatifical repose.

And neither, then, can we discover cause why
Christ may not be thought to have filled the office
of preacher to the buried tribes of the righteous,
and thus to have assumed that character which
he has never since laid aside, that of ' a minister
of the sanctuary, and of the true tabernacle which
the Lord pitched, and not man.' "[86]

This then is the doctrine of the Intermediate
state. Comfortable indeed to man in his feebleness is the thought, that even in this respect his
Lord hath prepared the way for him! The path
which connects this world of toil and sorrow
with one of songs and gladness, has been clearly
pointed out. It is still radiant with his Master's
footsteps, and His followers may tread it without fear. And if, when all things are bright
before him, he realizes this but feebly, yet to him
also there must come " a time to suffer and be
silent," when spiritual promises alone will be
able to satisfy the intense longings of his soul.
As man journeys onward through an evil world,
the glory of this lower life fades away — its hues
of beauty disappear — and are lost at last as the
clouds gather around his setting sun. Beautifully

[86] MELVILL'S *Sermons*, vol. i., p. 49.

indeed does one of England's Christian poets portray this change which passes over all things, thus weaning the Spirit away from this earth, and disposing it to look to Heaven.

> " Heaven lies about us in our infancy!
> Shades of the prison-house begin to close
>   Upon the growing Boy,
> But he beholds the light, and whence it flows,
>   He sees it in his joy;
> The Youth, who daily farther from the east
> Must travel still, is Nature's Priest,
>   And by the vision splendid
>   Is on his way attended;
> At length the man perceives it die away,
> And fade into the light of common day."[37]

Such is truly the sorrowful process of man's life. One by one the objects in which he had garnered up his affections pass away, until often in the gray twilight of his days he is left alone and desolate. Then indeed if he look around for sympathy, from the busy, earnest world about him there comes forth no response. Orestes-like he seeks for peace with a deeper yearning than that suppliant in the ancient Grecian Drama,[38]

[37] WORDSWORTH'S *Ode* — " Intimations of Immortality from Recollections of Early Childhood."

[38] ÆSCHYL. Eumen.

yet he seeks in vain. The flowers of his earthly
Paradise are faded, and its cisterns broken.
Memory lifts up her voice within him, like the
archangel's trump, summoning from their forgotten graves, thoughts and scenes which long since
had passed away. Their images rise up mournfully, as it were to mock him, for he knows that
the reality can never return. For him is reserved
only the lonely night, which stealing insensibly
on, is ever deepening its shadows about his path.

When therefore this world thus vanishes away
and life by its own vicissitudes has taught him
the lesson of his vanity—when nothing but evils
seem to " choke Time's groaning tide "—how
cheering is the thought, that the future yet remains to be his certain heritage! He raises his
eyes above the gathering darkness and the clouds
which surround him, and beholds beyond them,
that land which is always radiant with a celestial
glory. The past, with its sorrowful memories,
is forgotten, and he lives only in the anticipations
of the future. He is not driven forward to the
coming world without " knowing the things that
shall befall him there." He is sustained by the
" hope which maketh not ashamed." And thus

he passes along through the remaining days of
his pilgrimage, sharing in that spirit which the
old artists attempted to embody in their delinea-
tions of Faith when they represented her treading a rugged and thorny road, yet clasping the
Cross to her heart, and her eyes intently fixed
upon the calm, clear Heavens above. He feels
that Death shall only come like the Angel to
the Apostles, bursting the bars of his prison-
house, and leading him forth to the light and to
the day. His spirit pines within him for the
sweet waters of the River of Life. The voices
of the dead too, who have gone before, come
solemnly to his ears, as they urge him to press
onward to the promised land. There, his wanderings shall end, and the pilgrim staff be forever
cast aside. There he shall be at peace in the
mansions of rest, with the mighty army of patri-
archs and apostles, and confessors and martyrs,
who have already slept in the faith. Cheered
by a brighter manifestation of his Master's presence than can be his lot in this world, he shall
await his full reward, and the crown which shall
be given him at the last day. With what un-

wavering confidence may he then look up and say —

"Soon wilt Thou take us to Thy tranquil bower
    To rest one little hour,
Till Thine elect are number'd, and the grave
    Call Thee to come and save:
Then on thy bosom borne shall we descend,
    Again with earth to blend,
Earth all refin'd with bright supernal fires,
Tinctur'd with holy blood, and wing'd with pure desires.

Meanwhile, with every son and saint of Thine
    Along the glorious line,
Sitting by turns beneath Thy sacred feet
    We'll hold communion sweet,
Know them by look and voice, and thank them all
    For helping us in thrall,
For words of hope, and bright examples given
To show through moonless skies that there is light in
            Heaven."[39]

Thus ages shall glide by, until the history of this world is completed, and the number of the elect made up. Then our long expected Lord shall descend with a shout—the dust of each one of the saints be collected from the four winds, united again to its former partner, as the spirit comes forth from its resting-place, and all shall

[39] KEBLE'S *Easter Eve.*

gather around the throne of Him whom they followed while on earth, ready to receive the sentence — " Well done, good and faithful servants, enter ye into the joy of your Lord." This shall be the GREAT EASTER OF THE EARTH.

THE END.